The Origins of Intellect

A SERIES OF BOOKS IN PSYCHOLOGY

Editor: *Stanley Coopersmith*

The Origins of Intellect: Piaget's Theory

John L. Phillips, Jr.

BOISE STATE COLLEGE

W. H. FREEMAN AND COMPANY
San Francisco

Printed in the United States of America
Library of Congress Catalog Card Number: 69-13319

9 8 7 6 5 4 3 2

to my father

Preface

To the Teacher

When, just a few years ago, I was given the responsibility of planning a course in educational psychology, I very quickly made two decisions: (1) that it would be a course in psychology, not pedagogical methods, and (2) that it would have some focus.

I was surprised and delighted to find both the psychology and the focus in a collection of works that had been around for a long time. I had heard of Piaget, of course, for many years; but earlier, those who referred to him at all always did so with more than a modicum of condescending tolerance. Recently, however, I have detected a cognitive trend in the literature: more American psychologists have been directing their search for a theoretical model away from the laboratory rat and toward the electronic computer. I also discovered that many more writers are interested in Piaget and that most of their references to him are suffused with respect.

Consequently, I made an intensive study of Piaget; this book is the result of that study. It was originally a set of notes designed for use in teaching a class of upper-division students in educational psychology. The class was small enough to allow student participation, and my plan was to involve them as much as possible in the theoretical enterprise. It is not possible, of course, to do that in a book to the same extent that it can be done in a classroom, but the style of this book still reflects my original purpose. Often a problem is stated, and then the student is invited to think it through, using the same data as were available to Piaget. Many actual observations are reported in order to make that feasible.

Beyond that, this book is a general summary, at a relatively non-technical level, of Piaget's theory of the development of intelligence. It should serve very well the busy teacher of child psychology, child development, or educational psychology; of learning or psychological systems; or perhaps even of general psychology.

The book is *not* intended to be *The Compleat Piaget*. What I have done is to present Piaget's original theory together with enough illustrations of his research activities to give the theory meaning. The theory has only recently caught the interest of more than a few American psychologists; but it was actually promulgated many years ago, and although Piaget has refined his theoretical models and, along with others at Geneva and elsewhere, has produced more recent research than is included here, the basic theory remains essentially the same and can be presented most clearly in the context of its original development. Readers who have mastered these theoretical rudiments and wish to progress further will find an excellent review of Piaget's recent work, as well as a more thorough (and also more technical) discussion of the theory itself, plus a review of the studies of perception and moral concepts, in J. H. Flavell's *The Developmental Psychology of Jean Piaget* (1963).

Probably every teacher will have his own way of beginning the study of intellectual development in general and of Piaget's work in particular. My own way is to introduce my students to the theory of D. O. Hebb; because they have been encouraged to take a naturalistic view of human behavior, and I believe that Hebb has successfully demonstrated how—in principle, at least—"the ghost in the machine" can be dealt with in naturalistic terms. If the theoretical foundations of your course are cognitive to begin with, that will be of no concern to you, but I have felt the need of a bridge between the S-R paradigm with which I begin my course and the cognitive system that is Piaget. If you should feel the same need, you could put a Hebb book on reserve in your library: *A Textbook of Psychology* if your students are in teacher training, *The Organization of Behavior* if they are psychology majors. (The first edition of the *Textbook* is really better for your purpose than the second, in my opinion.)

The Origins of Intellect will serve nicely as a self-contained exposition of Piaget's theory. However, if you should wish to make that theory (and its practical implications) a substantial part of your course, you will want your students also to discuss it during class periods and perhaps to work with it outside of class. Often a greater involvement of students in the working through of scientific ideas can be fostered by supplementing their reading with graphic demonstrations of the tests of those ideas. As of this date I know of no suitable films of Piagetian tests, but there is a supply of subjects in nearly every community, and for demonstration purposes, students can administer the tests themselves. I usually assign at least one observation at each of three levels: Sensorimotor, Preoperational, and Concrete Operations. (The Formal Operations test described in the book requires more equipment than can be quickly and easily assembled by every student.) When making these assignments, students should be reminded that the most interesting results of the Piaget-type tests are the failures that occur; you might suggest that for each subject they try to find one test that he passes and one that he fails. And tell them to use each situation to learn as much as possible about the structure of the child's thought. They will find that they do indeed learn more from the failures than from the successes.

As a sequel to the unit on Piaget, two paperback volumes by Jerome Bruner seem to me especially appropriate: *The Process of Education* and *Toward a Theory of Instruction*. A careful examination of the journal articles cited in my bibliography will reveal an even more recent interest in the application of ideas similar to those of Piaget to problems in education. I was recently privileged to hear Robert M. Gagné's presidential address to Division 15 of the American Psychological Association. It was a paper entitled "Learning Hierarchies," which could, if one were so inclined, be used to explore my suggestion in Chapter V that a more thorough task analysis may be an avenue to progress in the teaching of operations. That paper has not been published, but the bibliography includes others that have. In this regard, I should mention that some of those articles have been reprinted in edited collections and that only a few have been listed with their original sources. The edited collections are rich mines of source materials.

To the Student

The chapter that I have called "Introduction" is primarily a quick survey of Piaget's entire theory, in preparation for a more detailed analysis of its parts. Very little of that chapter describes my approach to the teaching of the theory or relates it to the motivations of students. The following remarks are intended to remedy that omission.

Special Features and Study Suggestions

Because it is so often useful to make comparisons of one stage of development with another, I have continually sought opportunities for juxtaposition; so each topic heading refers to a sort of *mode* rather than to an exclusive category—e.g., in the section on Concrete Operations, much is said about Preoperational thinking in order that the differences between the two might be made clear. This means that the length of a section does not indicate very precisely the amount of attention that has been given to the topic announced in its heading; it means, too, that not all information pertinent to an announced topic may be found under that particular heading. But the comparison technique does build concepts efficiently, and that, after all, is our major objective.

In order to make the most of those conceptual acquisitions, you must weave them into a coherent pattern. It is the function of Chapter I to help you do just that. You are likely to find Chapter I exceedingly difficult the first time through, and it probably will not be very helpful by itself. But because the concepts introduced there are illustrated later on, the chapter can perform an organizing function if you will use it properly. A lecturer, of course, has more control of his students than an author does, and one of the ways in which I exercised that control when I was lecturing was to require, at the end of what is now Chapter IV, a careful review of Chapter I, so that the latter might serve as both an introduction to the theory and a summary of it. It is a difficult theory, and you will find Chapter I only vaguely intelligible on first reading; but I have presented it in the only intellectually honest way I could conceive, and the difficulty that you may have with it initially should heighten your satisfaction in the understanding that will be yours on the second try. The procedure that I recommend, and which has proven effective in my own classes, is as follows:

1. Read Chapter I with a set to remember where each topic is discussed (rather than for mastery of content).
2. Refer back to parts of it as you go through the other sections, this time digesting the content.
3. Reread the entire chapter after you have completed Chapter IV and before you begin Chapter V, striving now for an understanding of broad general relationships.

Piaget and Psychology

As you complete Chapters II, III, and IV and return for a review of Chapter I, a pattern will emerge, and you will comprehend better than you had at first my reasons for referring to "intelligence" as "the efficient processing of information" and for pointing out the compatibility of Piaget's system with Hebb's neurological theory. The lecture materials were selected and organized in this way because my reading of the literature reveals a marked increase in the amount of attention that psychologists have been giving recently to central mediating processes, and because my own interest has been moving in that direction. The change is epitomized by the choice of models in psychological theory. A shift seems to be occurring from stimulus-response connections to feedback loops—from the laboratory rat to the electronic computer.

My point about the shift from rat to computer is not that we have built computers more complex than the nervous system of a rat, but rather that in principle we *could* do so and, more important perhaps, that the programming of a computer demands a thorough analysis of the central organizing processes that control output—which, according to this view, is what psychology is all about. I hope that you will take from all this a conception of the human brain as a vastly complicated system for the storage and retrieval of information; a system that becomes more complex as it operates, and hence becomes capable of increasingly complex operations; a system that changes in ways that are at least to some degree similar to the constructions that Piaget has given us.

Reference by Future Writers

The publications of the Geneva school constitute by far the largest repository of knowledge about the cognitive development of children that is available anywhere; students of psychology should be familiar with Piaget's theory even if it turns out to be basically wrong, because it will undoubtedly serve as a base for many future studies of children's thinking.

Understanding for Its Own Sake

If Piaget is correct, understanding is reinforcing in and of itself. If so, your study of this book should be rewarded not only by its effect on your subsequent reading about children, but more directly by its effect on your interaction with them. You should experience a satisfaction similar to that of an anthropologist who has been studying a pre-literate culture and, after much intensive effort, develops the ability to see the world as the natives do, and thus at last really to communicate with them.

Practical Implications

Satisfactions of that kind should be sufficient unto themselves—particularly for people who will be in daily contact with children; but if you are a prospective teacher, counselor, or school psychologist, you are doubtless eager to find additional rewards related to your professional activities.

If you were to review the first four chapters with that in mind, you might very well find for yourself some important implications of the theory for educators in general and teachers in particular. Your review time, however, might better be spent in a concentrated effort to understand the theory as such. After you have done that, you will be ready to consider in Chapter V some of the implications of the theory for those who would intervene in the developmental process.

Acknowledgments

Whatever success may have been achieved here must be attributed to the cooperation of many people. Prominent among them were the scholars who discussed theoretical questions with me, gave me leads to pertinent literature, or both: Hans Aebli of Universität Konstanz in Germany, the staff of the Arithmetic Project at the University of Illinois, Jerome Bruner of Harvard University, Stanley Coopersmith of the University of California at Davis, Philip Cowan of the University of California at Berkeley, J. A. Easley of the University of Illinois, John Flavell of the University of Minnesota, J. McV. Hunt of the University of Illinois, Frank Jennings of *Saturday Review*, Neil Kephart of Glen Haven Achievement Center in Fort Collins, Jonas Langer of the University of California at Berkeley, G. Matthews of the Nuffield Foundation in London, O. K. Moore of the University of Pittsburgh, Adrien Pinard of the University of Montreal in Canada, William Sickles of the American Institute for Research, Irving Sigel of The Merrill-Palmer Institute, The United States Office of Education, and Burton White of Harvard University. Jerry Young of the

Boise State College Department of Mathematics graciously consented to review the section on concrete operations from the point of view of his discipline.

Two of these scholars have been especially influential: Philip Cowan, whose reaction to the original draft of the manuscript encouraged me to continue; and Stanley Coopersmith, whose careful and insightful reading of subsequent revisions had important effects in critical places.

I also wish to express my appreciation for the competence, industry, and gracious cooperation of the library staff at Boise State College and of my wife, Elaine, who gave generously of both typing skills and moral support.

Finally, it should be noted that this book was born during a summer at Berkeley—a summer that I would have been unable to spend there without a grant from the National Science Foundation.

December 1968

John L. Phillips, Jr.

Contents

I

Introduction

I

Introduction

Dear Reader:

Despite the inference that you may have drawn from its title, this chapter is not the beginning of the book. It begins in the Preface.

It is true that a preface always contains some information that is of no interest to most readers, but the Preface is more important in this book than in most. It explains the structure of the book, and that structure is essential to efficient study of the main body of the text.

John L. Phillips, Jr.

Piaget and His Methods

Jean Piaget is a Swiss psychologist who was trained in zoology and whose major interests are essentially philosophical. He and his associates have been publishing their findings on the development of cognitive processes in children since 1927, and have accumulated the largest store of factual and theoretical observations extant today.

Piaget is often criticized because his method of investigation, though somewhat modified in recent years, is still largely clinical. He observes the child's surroundings and his behavior, formulates a hypothesis concerning the structure that underlies and includes them both, and then tests that hypothesis by altering the surroundings slightly — by rearranging the materials, by posing the problem in a different way, or even by overtly suggesting to the subject a response different from the one predicted by the theory.

An example of the method is the investigation of the preoperational child's conception of velocity. The child observes the movement of an object through points A, B, C, and D. He reports that the object passed through point D "after" point A and that it took "more time" to get from A to C than from A to B. From this it might reasonably be inferred that the child's conception of temporal succession and duration is the same as that of an adult. But the investigation doesn't stop there. The subject is then presented with the simultaneous movements of *two* objects. The investigator systematically varies the actual distance through which each of the objects move, their time in transit, and their initial and terminal positions relative to one another. When that is done, the child no longer responds as an adult would in similar circumstances. For example, if two objects move simultaneously — i.e., if they start simultaneously and stop simultaneously — but at different velocities, the child will deny their simultaneity of movement. To him, each moving object has a different "time," and one that is a function of the *spatial* features of the display.

The systematic manipulation of variables illustrated by that example is certainly in the tradition of classical experimental science. The example, however, is drawn from one of the more rigorous of the studies done by Piaget and his colleagues. Their investigations often begin with naturalistic observations and continue as an interaction between the child and the "experimenter" — an interaction in which each varies his behavior in response to that of the other.

Another example may serve to illustrate the point: it is an "experiment" designed to reveal the child's conception of number. The child is presented with an assemblage of coins and a large number of flowers; he is asked to tell how many flowers he can purchase with the coins if the price of each flower is one coin. Here is a transcript of one such encounter:

> Gui (four years, four months) put 5 flowers opposite 6 pennies, then made a one-for-one exchange of 6 pennies for 6 flowers (taking the extra flower from the reserve supply). The pennies were in a row and the flowers bunched together: "What have we done? — *We've exchanged them.*—Then is there the same number of flowers and pennies? —*No.*—Are there more on one side? —*Yes.*—Where? —*There* (pennies). (The exchange was again made, but this time the pennies were put in a pile and the flowers in a row.) Is there the same number of flowers and pennies? —*No.*—Where are there more? —*Here* (flowers).—And here (pennies)? —*Less.*[1]

This shifting of experimental procedures to fit the responses of a particular subject makes replication difficult, and the results may be especially susceptible to the "experimenter effect."[2] The reader who feels impelled to criticize Piaget's method is in good company. But before becoming too enthusiastic a critic, he should be sure to note the deliberate effort that is made to give the child opportunities for responses that would *not* fit the theory. He should also keep in mind Piaget's epistomological position that knowledge is action.[3] The subject is continually acting. His actions are structured, and they are also to some extent autonomous. The investigator must therefore continually change his line of attack if he is to follow those actions and to discern their underlying structure.

---

[1] Jean Piaget and Alina Szeminska, *The Child's Conception of Number*, translated by C. Gattegno and F. M. Hodgson, New York: Humanities Press, 1952. (Original French edition, 1941.)

[2] Sometimes called the "Rosenthal effect," after R. Rosenthal, who in several recent studies has demonstrated that even in apparently objective experimental situations, the experimenter can influence the subject's behavior in a number of subtle and unacknowledged ways (facial expression, tone of voice, etc.). Even rat subjects perform better for experimenters who expect them to do so, presumably because of differences in handling by different experimenters (R. Rosenthal and K. L. Fade, "The Effect of Experimenter Bias on the Performance of the Albino Rat," *Behavioral Science*, 1963, pp. 183–189, and R. Rosenthal and R. Lawson, "A Longitudinal Study of Experimenter Bias on the Operant Learning of Laboratory Rats," *Journal of Psychiatric Research*, 1964). An interesting study of the experimenter effect in humans is R. Rosenthal and L. Jacobson, *Pygmalion in the Classroom*, 1968.

[3] "Action" need not necessarily be motor.

Relation to Other Theories

The early work of Piaget's Geneva group was given considerable attention in the scholarly press, but because psychology, especially in the United States, was at that time dominated by associationistic theories of learning and by content-oriented psychometrics, their work generated little interest.

The current explosion of interest in Piaget's work is an expression of the same concern that produced Hebb's neurological theory and the various contemporary models of the brain as an information-processing system. That concern was probably occasioned not so much by a sudden increase in dissatisfaction with existing theories as by the advances that have taken place recently in neurophysiology and computer engineering.

In any case, Piaget's observations and formulations are today a definite focus of theoretical and professional interest in psychology. The theory is cognitive rather than associationistic;[4] it is concerned primarily with structure rather than content—with *how* the mind works rather than with *what* it does. It is concerned more with understanding than with prediction and control of behavior.

These remarks can of course only be made by way of emphasis, for we can never know the *how* except through the *what;* we can only infer central processes from the behaviors that they organize. An affirmation of one kind of analysis does not necessarily imply a negation of the other. There are conflicts between them, but often the dissonance is more apparent than real, and a careful reading of both kinds of analysis often reveals a harmony that could not be seen at first glance. Hebb's work especially has shown us the way here, and his *magnum opus*[5] is highly recommended to the serious student of psychological theory.

Before turning to the first of Piaget's periods of development, let

---

[4] A cognitive theory is concerned especially with central organizing processes in higher animals, and it recognizes a partial autonomy of these processes, such that the animal becomes an actor upon, rather than simply a reactor to its environment. Actually, the opposite of all this, the so-called associationist doctrine, is to some extent a straw man; for excepting B. F. Skinner, who abjures all theories, there is probably no prominent psychologist today who does not explicitly recognize the importance of mediating processes. But there is a difference in emphasis, and like most straw men this one serves the purpose of accentuating that difference.

[5] D. O. Hebb, *The Organization of Behavior*, New York: John Wiley & Sons, Inc., 1949.

us take a quick overview of the theory, in preparation for the more detailed account that will follow in Chapters II, III, and IV.

Overview of Piaget's Theory

Structure and Function

The basic underlying idea is that *functions* remain invariant but that *structures* change systematically as the child develops. This change in structures is development.

Another term found often in Piaget's writing is *content*, by which he means observable stimuli and responses. We may talk in abstract terms about "function" and "structure," but as soon as we cite an actual example, we must deal also with content.

Such an example might be: "A baby looks at a rattle and picks it up." The structure of this event includes the means (looking, reaching, grasping) and the end (stimulation from the object in hand). Each of these is related to the other, and it is this relatedness that Piaget calls "structure."[6] The function of the baby's act is *adaptation*—i.e., the reception and registration of inputs, and the accommodation of each element to the others. "Content" refers to the patterns of input and output.

The term "structure" refers to the systemic properties of an event; it encompasses all aspects of an act, both internal and external. "Function," however, refers to biologically inherited modes of interacting with the environment—modes that are characteristic of such integrations in all biological systems. With reference to intelligence, this inherited "functional nucleus" imposes "certain necessary and irreducible conditions"[7] on structures. There are two basic functions: *organization* and *adaptation*. Every act is organized, and the dynamic aspect of organization is adaptation.

Discontinuities in structure continually arise out of the continuous action of invariant functions. Throughout the developmental period, functions are permanent. But structures are transitory; if they weren't, there would be no development.

---

[6] Each by itself has its own structure, too. See also footnote 9, p. 9.

[7] Piaget, *The Origins of Intelligence in Children*, translated by Margaret Cook, New York: International Universities Press, 1952, p. 3. (Original French edition, 1936.)

Assimilation

If we think of the human brain as a machine for processing information, we must realize not only that it is an exceedingly complex machine, but also that its internal structure is continually changing. We are reminded of Hebb's notion that the precise pattern of cortical activity initiated by an incoming stimulus is a function not only of the pattern of that stimulus, but also of what is already going on in the brain. (See pp. 16–17.) This is close to what Piaget means by assimilation.

Assimilation occurs whenever an organism utilizes something from its environment and incorporates it. A biological example would be the ingestion of food. The food is changed in the process, and so is the organism. Psychological processes are similar in that the pattern in the stimulation is changed and, again, so is the organism.

In introductory psychology courses it is demonstrated that even the perception of an object is not a faithful reproduction of a stimulus pattern. For example, our perception of objects remains the same even though changes in distance, angle of view, and amount of light produce rather striking differences in the size, shape, brightness, and hue of the image that is actually projected onto the retina. (This is, of course, the phenomenon known as "object constancy.") Beyond that, objects are invested with meaning—i.e., they are categorized in terms of such dimensions as familiarity, threat, and beauty. In sum, the input is changed to fit the existing "mediating" processes. The organism is always active, and its cognitions—even perceptions of its immediate surroundings—are as much a function of this activity as they are of the physical properties of the environment.

Accommodation

But at the same time that the input is being changed by the mediating processes, the mediating processes are being changed by the input. Object constancy, which was just used to illustrate the former, can also be used to illustrate the latter. Each "correction" that is applied by the brain to a retinal image had to be learned—i.e., the mediating processes that act upon the input have themselves been shaped by that input.

Take size constancy, for example. Think of the thousands upon thousands of times that the size of an image on your own retina has covaried with distance from you to the object. Other inputs, such as proprioceptive ones that arise as you have approached the object, and the temporal relations among these, all have contributed to the changing of patterns of mediation.[8] The mechanism by which these changes occur Piaget calls accommodation.

Functional Invariants:
Assimilation and Accommodation

Accommodation and assimilation are called "functional invariants" because they are charactistic of all biological systems, regardless of the varying contents of these systems. They are not, however, always in balance, one with the other.

Temporary imbalances occur when a child is imitating (accommodation over assimilation) and when he is playing (assimilation over accommodation). Behavior is most adaptive when accommodation and assimilation are in balance, but such a balance is always temporary, because the process of adaptation reveals imperfections in the system. (See the section below on *Equilibration*.)

Schemata

As I mentioned previously, cognitive development consists of a succession of changes, and the changes are structural.

The structural units in Piaget's system are called *schemata*, which is the plural of *schema*. Schemata are roughly equivalent to the "mediating processes" of Hebb and others.[9] They form a kind of framework onto which incoming sensory data can fit—indeed must fit; but it is a framework that is continually changing its shape, the better to assimilate those data.

Figure 1.1 summarizes some of these relationships.

---

[8] There is recent evidence that some of this organization is innate (T. G. R. Bower, "The Visual World of Infants," *Scientific American*, vol. 215, no. 6 (December 1966), pp. 80–92, and "Phenomenal Identity and Form Perception in an Infant," *Journal of Perception and Psychophysics*, 1967, pp. 74–76).

[9] Actually, Piaget's schemata include also the stimulus that triggers the mediating processes and the overt behavior that presumably is organized by them. Moreover, this whole process can involve interactions among schemata; i.e., they can assimilate each other. Schema, then, is the generic unit of structure. The earliest schemata are relatively simple, but with continued functioning, it becomes increasingly appropriate to consider such synonyms as "strategies," "plans," "transformation rules," "expectancies," etc.

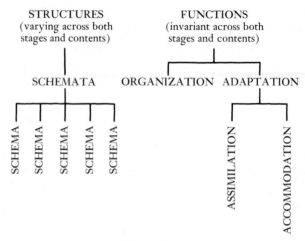

Figure 1.1

Equilibration

One concept that is *not* represented by the diagram is that of *equilibration*. The word will not be used again in this book, but the idea to which it refers should be kept constantly in mind while studying Piaget's theory in subsequent chapters, for it was the inspiration for the theory in the first place and remains its overarching principle.

The idea is that structures continually move toward a state of equilibrium, and when a state of relative equilibrium has been attained, the structure is sharper, more clearly delineated, than it had been previously. But that very sharpness points up inconsistencies and gaps in the structure that had never been salient before. Each equilibrium state therefore carries with it the seeds of its own destruction, for the child's activities are thenceforth directed toward reducing those inconsistencies and closing those gaps.

The process by which structures change from one state to another is called *equilibration*, and the result of that process is a state of *equilibrium*. Equilibrium is always dynamic and is never absolute, but the achievement of a relatively equilibrated system of actions is the expected conclusion of each of the several units of development listed in Table I.

Developmental Units

Piaget conceives intellectual development as a continual process of organization and reorganization of structure, each new organization integrating the previous one into itself. Although this process is continuous, its results are discontinuous; they are qualitatively different from time to time. Because of that, Piaget has chosen to break the total course of development into units called *periods, subperiods,* and *stages.* Note carefully, however, that each of these cross sections of development is described in terms of the *best* the child can do at that time. Many previously learned behaviors will occur even though he is capable of new and better ones.

Let us now examine the theory in detail, following the outline that appears in Table I; then, having analyzed each unit in its turn, we'll look back and see whether it is possible to discern the unifying threads that run through all of them.

Table I. Units in the Development of Intelligence According to Piaget

Sensorimotor Period—six stages	
Exercising the ready-made sensorimotor schemata	0–1 mo.[10]
Primary circular reactions	1–4 mo.
Secondary circular reactions	4–8 mo.
Coordination of secondary schemata	8–12 mo.
Tertiary circular reactions	12–18 mo.
Invention of new means through mental combinations	18–24 mo.
Concrete Operations Period[11]	
Preoperational subperiod	2–7 yr.
Concrete operations subperiod[12]	7–11 yr.
Formal Operations Period	11–15 yr.

[10] All age ranges are approximations. In children of any age range one can usually find manifestations of more than one stage or period. The important point is that the same *sequence* of development occurs in every child.

[11] Because Piaget and his co-workers have not been consistent in their indexing, the reader may encounter slightly different classifications in other readings, especially in discussions of middle childhood. More refined classifications have been devised, notably some that include stages within subperiods, but those will not be used in this book.

[12] Because it might seem confusing to use the same words in a generic category and in one of its subcategories, I suggest that the reader look upon the former as a unit that includes preparation for concrete operations, and the latter as a sub-unit that includes only the culmination of that development.

II

Sensorimotor Period
(0-2 years)

The six stages

> *Exercising the ready-made sensorimotor schemata
> (0–1 mo.)*
>
> *Primary circular reactions (1–4 mo.)*
>
> *Secondary circular reactions (4–8 mo.)*
> > *Intention and means-end relations*
> > *"Motor meaning"*
> > *Incorporation of new objects into existing
> > schemata*
> > *Object permanence and the construction
> > of space*
>
> *Coordination of the secondary schemata (8–12 mo.)*
> > *Intention and means-end relations*
> > *Sign meaning*
> > *Incorporation of new objects into existing
> > schemata*
> > *Object permanence and the construction of space*
> > *Causality*
>
> *Tertiary circular reactions (12–18 mo.)*
> > *Intention and means-end relations*
> > *Object permanence, space and time*
> > *Causality*

II

Sensorimotor Period

Cognitive development probably begins before birth, but since Piaget's observations start at that point, that is where we shall begin. To those who are preparing for some kind of work in public education, even that may seem too early; but remember that our objective is to understand intellectual development. Given that objective, the earliest adaptations must be recognized as fundamental. Later developments are built upon foundations laid in infancy.

It is sometimes useful, for purposes of exposition, to point out similarities between an unfamiliar theory and one that is familiar. Piaget might say that when this is done, the unfamiliar theory is "assimilated to" the familiar one. Because most American students of psychology are familiar with the work of D. O. Hebb of McGill University; because his theory is the respected contribution of a rigorous methodological behaviorist, and is nonetheless compatible with the kind of views advanced by Piaget; and because in particular he emphasizes the importance of "early learning" to intellectual development—for all of these reasons, this chapter, especially, will feature occasional references to Hebb's theory. The next four paragraphs constitute a brief review of that theory. Readers already familiar with the theory may skip them with impunity; those who are not may supplement them with profit.[1]

The evolution of complex organisms has necessarily been accompanied by that of complex behavioral control systems. A one-celled animal reacts in a severely limited way to its immediate environment; a higher animal has an elaborate repertory of responses to a wide variety of stimuli. But that elaboration and that flexibility are achieved at the expense of biological simplicity; such an animal is composed of many parts—some specialized for reception of information from the environment, others for actions upon it. A higher animal must therefore possess a transmission device that integrates the activities of the parts.

But once a transmission device has developed, the way is open to an additional development; that of *alternative connections* within the system. Thus not only are the higher animal's reception and response capabilities complex, but so are the mechanisms that relate those capabilities. Relations between stimulus and response are different for higher and lower animals. A lower animal is "sense-dominated"; its response to a specific input from the environment is immediate and predictable. A higher animal's behavior, however, is controlled not only by inputs from its immediate surroundings, but also by "mediating processes" within the transmission system—processes that are largely the result of previous functioning of the system. Therefore, the higher animal's response to a specific input is not necessarily immediate, and it is not predictable merely from knowledge of the current input pattern. To predict the behavior of a higher animal, it is necessary to know something about its mediating processes. In order to predict a human subject's response to a combination of digits—say "8" and "2"—I would have to know what he had learned about arithmetic before he ever came into my laboratory; whether he had in the immediate past been instructed to add, to subtract, to multiply, or to divide; whether he had a generalized set to follow directions; and so on. A person's behavior is determined both by the sensory input at the moment, *and* by the

---

[1] The original statement of Hebb's theory appears in *The Organization of Behavior*, New York, John Wiley & Sons, Inc., 1949, and a more recent but less thorough treatment in either the first (1958) or the second (1966) edition of *A Textbook of Psychology*, Philadelphia: W. B. Saunders Co.

way in which his "transmission system"[2] has been organized.[3]

According to Hebb, that organization has its roots in the repetitive patterning of inputs. Although some parts of the transmission system (reflexive mechanisms, for example) are pre-empted by the genes, most are available for organization into subsystems that have not been pre-determined. When patterned input first occurs, there is random activity within the system; but patterns that are initially random gradually become reliable representations of the outer world.[4] They also become the interchangeable elements of new, more elaborate patterns. It takes many, many repetitions to form one of the elemental patterns; but later on, a super-pattern may be formed in an instant. Learning in the adult, then, is different from that in the infant, but it cannot occur unless "early learning" has already been accomplished.

Like Hebb, Piaget has conceived a more comprehensive interpretation of the period of infancy than have most workers in the field. Few of them have dealt with infancy as a period of intellectual growth at all. But Piaget shows how the necessary processes of symbolic intelligence begin developing at birth, and how a shift occurs later from motor symbols to conceptual symbols. Some theorists have seen adult intelligence as an elaboration of motor symbols; others have dealt only with conceptual symbols; but Piaget has shown that one grows out of the other.[5]

---

[2] By this time, the "transmission system" has of course acquired the functions of storage and retrieval of information. In any event, the term is mine, not Hebb's.

[3] Plus other factors that, for our purposes, may be disregarded.

[4] Hebb calls these basic patterns "cell assemblies," and he postulates that their reliability gradually becomes established through the growth of a "synaptic knob" that gets a little bigger each time there is simultaneous activity in the two neurons served by a particular synapse. Each "growth" increases the area of contact between the two cells, thereby lowering resistance to subsequent transmission across that synapse.

That such "knobs" do exist is a matter of fact; but since Hebb's theory was published, many other facts have accumulated which suggest that the memory mechanism is basically chemical. There is even some evidence (Dingman and Sporn, 1961; Hyden, 1961; Katz and Halstead, 1950; Schmitt, 1962; Halstead, 1968) that the locus of change is not in the synapse at all, but in RNA molecules—probably in the neural cell body or internal portions of the cellular membrane. Such speculations need not concern us here, however; for a theory may be infirmed at one level of analysis and confirmed at others, and Hebb's conceptions have in many ways held up very well. For us the important point is that, whatever the neurological mechanism, early experience is of critical importance to later development. There is also evidence (Fantz, 1965; Hubel and Wiesel, 1965; Bower, 1966, 1967) of some coding mechanisms that are apparently innate; but it is clear that such mechanisms must, at least in the human, be richly supplemented by patterned inputs.

[5] Another writer who has suggested a partial integration of Hebb and Piaget is J. McV. Hunt (*Intelligence and Experience*, New York: Ronald Press Co., 1961).

The Six Stages

Probably no other feature of Piaget's system has been opposed with so much vigor as his conception of *stages*. "There are so many influences on a child's development," say the critics, "how could they possibly combine to produce the same 'stage' of development in every child of a given age?"

Piaget has not given a completely satisfactory answer to those critics. Nevertheless, the concept of stage can be useful if we keep in mind three things: (1) that different children may pass through the sequence of stages at different rates, (2) that each stage is named for the process that has most recently become operative, even though others may be operating at the same time,[6] and (3) that each is the formation of a total structure that includes its predecessors within it as necessary substructures.

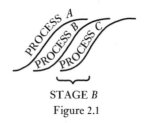

STAGE *B*

Figure 2.1

Notice that in Figure 2.1 the period within the brackets is labeled "Stage *B*," even though Process *A* is in full operation and Process *C* has begun to develop. For a "gifted" child, all these curves would be steeper, closer together, and shifted to the left (the processes develop faster), and for a "retarded" child, they would be flatter, farther apart, and shifted to the right (the processes develop more slowly). For each child, however, Piaget maintains that the *sequence* remains the same. And finally, with the exception noted in footnote 6, Stages *A*, *B*, and *C* do not coexist as independent systems; rather, *B* includes *A*, and *C* includes both *A* and *B*. The overall structure that characterizes any given stage is an integration of those that preceded it, and the achievements of that stage are preparations for those of the next.

---

[6] Other processes do function in every stage except the first.

Stage 1. Exercising the Ready-made Sensorimotor Schemata (0-1 month)

The infant is born with a number of sensorimotor mechanisms "wired in." (A familiar term for them is "reflexes.") The infant makes orienting responses to light or sound; his hands grasp an object placed in his palm; he sucks when his lips are touched; he vocalizes, waves his arms, etc., in response to any strong stimulus. This is not a complete list of innate mechanisms; however, the list need not be extended here, for Piaget is not interested in hereditary organizations as such, but rather in the alterations that occur in them as the child interacts with his environment.

The first stage may therefore be passed over lightly. Keep in mind, however, that according to Hebb, cell assemblies are being formed during this period that will enter into, and in fact be basic to the development of, more complex functioning later on.

Stage 2. Primary Circular Reactions (1-4 months)

Piaget, too, notes that the second stage, Primary Circular Reactions,[7] is based upon the development that takes place in the first. It is marked by variations in the schemata as more and more stimulus patterns are assimilated, by coordination of various schemata as functional relationships are developed among them (e.g., hearing and looking at the same object, seeing and reaching-grasping the same object, reaching-grasping and sucking the same object), and by perceptual recognition of objects as a result of repeated stimulation.

The reader may recall Hebb's suggestion that perception is a function of organized cell assemblies, and that each cell assembly results from repetition of a particular stimulus pattern—e.g., a particular odor, slope, angle, or curve.[8] Piaget's observations indicate that something of this kind must be going on. "Just looking" becomes "looking in order to see." This is inferred from the infant's differential responses to

---

[7] They are called "primary" because they are centered on the infant's body rather than on external objects, "circular" because they are endlessly repeated. The pattern is this: (1) the child stumbles onto an act that produces a new experience and (2) repeats the act to reproduce the experience.

[8] *The Organization of Behavior*, pp. 80–84, and *A Textbook of Psychology* (1st ed.), 1958, p. 105.

various objects. Originally, he reacts to all objects indiscriminately; later, he looks more at some than others, smiles at some more than others, etc. Reaching and touching is repeated many times with apparent pleasure. Sucking is continued on some objects, discontinued on others.

During this period, the behavior of the child begins to be centered on *objects;* but to him there is no objective reality—no general space or time, no permanence of objects. There are only *events*—i.e., components of the child's own functioning. When an object in his field of vision disappears, it ceases to exist. Without permanence of objects, there can be no general space, though there may be visual space, auditory space, tactual space, etc. *Time* is similarly limited to that which encompasses a single event, such as moving a hand from leg to face, feeling the nipple and beginning to suck, or hearing a sound and seeing its source.

Overt activity is necessary to the development that occurs in this stage. Piaget noted that one of his children was retarded in "hand-watching" coordination. This child had been born in the winter, and to give her as much sun as possible it was necessary to bundle her in blankets, which prevented her from engaging in the activity from which "hand-watching" develops.

I have noticed that those who write about "early experience" tend to cite this emphasis on motor activity as an important difference between Piaget and Hebb, who stresses the effects of sensory input. I must confess that I am a little puzzled by this, because it seems to me that Hebb makes explicit his concern for the possible contribution of overt behavior. The reader may remember that he postulates "motor loops" for many of his cell assemblies. There may be a difference, but it doesn't seem to me to be a significant one.

To summarize: during the second stage there is progress toward integration of the biologically given patterns of the infant into habits and perceptions. Note carefully that these changes occur simultaneously through the reciprocal effects of the functions that Piaget calls accommodation and assimilation.

Stage 3. Secondary Circular Reactions (4-8 months)

The stage of secondary circular reactions is so called because the "reactions" are the amalgamation of schemata developed earlier (hence the term "secondary") and because they are repetitive and self-rein-forcing[9] (which makes them "circular"). A useful prototype might be "shaking a rattle to hear the noise." The reaching-and-grasping and the listening-to-the-noise have been amalgamated into a new "circular" reaction.

Intention and Means-End Relations

Many of Piaget's interpretive comments have been deleted from the following quotation. Can you identify the behaviors from which he infers "intention"?

Observation 94:
[At three months, five days] Lucienne shakes her bassinet by moving her legs violently (bending and unbending them, etc.), which makes the cloth dolls swing from the hood. Lucienne looks at them smiling, and recommences at once.... The next day, I present the dolls: Lu-cienne immediately moves, shakes her legs, but this time without smil-ing.... At age three months, eight days, I find Lucienne swinging her dolls. An hour later I make them move slightly: Lucienne looks at them, smiles, stirs a little, then resumes looking at her hand as she was doing shortly before. A chance movement disturbs the dolls: Lucienne again looks at them and this time shakes herself with regularity. She stares at the dolls, barely smiles, and moves her legs vigorously and thor-oughly....

At three months, thirteen days, Lucienne looks at her hand with more coordination than usual. In her joy at seeing her hand come and go between her face and the pillow, she shakes herself in front of this hand as when faced by the dolls. Now this reaction of the shaking appears to remind her of the dolls, which she looks at immediately, as though she foresaw their movement.... At age three months, sixteen days, as soon as I suspend the dolls she immediately shakes them, with-out smiling, with precise and rhythmical movements with quite an interval between shakes.... At four months, four days, in a new bas-sinet, she moves her loins violently in order to shake the hood. At four months, thirteen days, she moves her legs very rapidly while looking at the festoons on the bassinet hood: as soon as she see them again, after a pause, she begins once more....

At four months, twenty-seven days, Lucienne is lying in her bas-sinet. I hang a doll from the hood over her feet. This immediately sets

---

[9] The term "reinforcement," here and throughout the book, is intended to imply only an empirical relationship, not a hypothetical construct. The empirical fact is that the child does repeat the activity without being exposed to any "reinforcing stimulus" that is external to it.

in motion the schema of shaking. Her feet reach the doll and give it
a violent movement, which Lucienne surveys with delight. Afterward
she looks at her motionless foot for a second, then recommences....

At five months, eighteen days, I place the doll at different heights,
sometimes to the left, sometimes to the right: Lucienne tries to reach
it with her foot, and then, when she has succeeded, she shakes it....[10]

Before he will say that an act is *intentional*, Piaget requires that it
show three characteristics:

1. Object-centered orientation.
2. Intermediate acts (means) preceding the goal act (end).
3. Deliberate adaptation to a new situation.

It is clear from Observation 94 that Lucienne's behavior meets the
first two of these requirements. As for the third, Piaget does not give
us an operational definition of "deliberate" adaptation, but he apparently infers it from the often serious visage, the pause between presen-
tation of the stimulus and initiation of the response, and the constant
end-effect—in this example, the swinging of the dolls.

But the schemata underlying this behavior are only the beginnings
of "intention and means-ends separation," because in them the relation
of means to end is fortuitous. The infant apparently comes to anticipate
an interesting spectacle whenever he produces a certain action; but
does this meet the criterion of "deliberateness"? Later on the action
and the effect will be clearly differentiated, and both will be subsumed
under a strong intentional schema. The difference is one of degree,
but it is a difference; intention and means-end separation do *not* appear
full-blown in Stage 3.

Motor Meaning

Here is another series of observations. The inference in this example will probably be a little more difficult to grasp than the preceding
one. See if you can tease it out.

Observation 107:
At age five months, three days, Lucienne tries to grasp a spool suspended above her by means of elastic bands.... She manages to touch
but not to grasp them. Having shaken them fortuitously, she then

---

[10]*The Origins of Intelligence in Children,* translated by Margaret Cook, New
York: International Universities Press, 1952, pp. 157–159. (Original French edition,
1936.)

breaks off to shake herself a moment while looking at them, but then she resumes her attempts at grasping.... Why has she broken off in order to shake herself a few seconds? It was not in order to shake the spool, because she did not persevere and because she was busy with something else at the moment; neither was it in order to facilitate her attempts at grasping....

At age five months, ten days, Lucienne again relapses into states identical to those with the dolls. At age six months, five days, she shakes herself several times in succession. It is an outline of some action suggested by this sight.... At six months, twelve days, Lucienne perceives from a distance two celluloid parrots attached to a chandelier. These she had sometimes had on the hood of her bassinet. As soon as she sees them, she definitely but briefly shakes her legs, but without trying to act upon them from a distance.

.... At six months, nineteen days, it suffices that she catches sight of her dolls from a distance (these are dolls that she had previously learned to swing with her hands) for her to outline the movement of swinging them with her hand.... From seven months, twenty-seven days, certain highly familiar situations no longer set in motion secondary circular reactions, but simply outlines of the schemata. Thus when seeing a doll that she actually had swung many times, Lucienne limits herself to opening and closing her hands or shaking her legs, but very briefly and without real effort.... It is only a sort of acknowledgment.[11]

Note especially (1) the increasing *brevity* of the motor response as the pattern develops and (2) the apparent *lack of intention;* the action appears instead to be *representing* the object. I submit that the responses that the child has made to an object are, in effect, its *meaning.* For you and me, the meaning of an object or event consists entirely of implicit responses and Hebbian mediating processes. For the child, these responses become increasingly covert as he grows older, but his central processes are not yet sufficiently elaborated or organized for meaning to be "mental." It is rather, as Piaget puts it, "an outline of some action suggested by this sight..."[12]

---

[11] *Ibid.*, pp. 186–187. Again, most of the interpretations have been deleted.

[12] "Motor meaning" (the term used as the heading for this section) is my own term, not Piaget's. He speaks of "motor recognition" and of "recognitory assimilation"; but the initial referent of each of these is the very first differentiation of responses in Stage 1 (*Ibid.*, pp. 36 ff.) — i.e., the barest beginning of the differential (to various objects) responses that become clearly observable later, in Stage 2. (See above reference, p. 21.) Motor meaning is more complex, and does not appear until Stage 3.

Incorporation of New Objects into Existing Schemata

Related to this "outline of action" is the behavior described in the following brief excerpt:

> *Observation 110:*
> [At three months, twenty-nine days] Laurent sees for the first time the paper knife. He grasps and looks at it, but only for a moment. Afterward he immediately swings it with his right hand as he does all objects grasped. He then rubs it by chance against the wicker of the bassinet and tries to produce the sound heard as though the knife were the rattle he has used for this purpose. It then suffices that I place the the object in his left hand for him to shake it in the same fashion . . . .[13]

Piaget refers to the knife as an *aliment* for habitual schemata. By swinging objects, shaking them, and rubbing them against the side of the crib, new objects are incorporated into existing schemata.

Object Permanence and the Construction of Space

You and I are wont to assume that the real world is there, that we apprehend it as it is (assuming that there is nothing wrong with our sensory apparatus), and that's all there is to it! Actually, however, as Hebb, especially, has been at great pains to point out, some of the most rudimentary perceptions are achieved only after a great deal of experience.

The inference that an object has a *permanence* beyond our immediate perception of it comes about even more slowly; it does not even begin in the average child until the stage we are discussing now.[14] We know that it does begin at this stage because of a particular change in his behavior in a certain kind of situation—namely, one in which he has been attending to an object and it is suddenly removed from his visual field. Before, he would simply shift his attention to something else; but now he may search for the absent object.

---

[13] *Ibid.*, p. 197.

[14] Psychiatrists have coined the term, "separation anxiety" to refer to the distress that is occasioned by the absence of the mother. But how can the child be distressed about being separated from her if she does not exist when she is not present? The answer is, he can't; and in point of fact, separation anxiety does not occur in Stages 1 or 2. Its development is correlated, as one might suspect, with that of object permanence; until then, it is literally a case of "out of sight, out of mind."

Children in Stage 3 do in fact engage in some searching for absent objects, but at this age it is of very brief duration, and it is confined to one modality—e.g., a felt object will be groped for but not looked for, and a seen object will be looked for but not groped for.

Related to the permanence of objects is the development of space and time dimensions. Whereas space had previously been confined to that mediated by a single modality, or even locality, of input (e.g., visual, tactile-kinesthetic, or buccal), in the third stage these various spaces become organized into what Piaget calls a "groupment."

This *grouping* comes about as a result of the infant's increasing coordination of seeing, reaching-grasping, and sucking. As the child becomes more adept at these coordinations, he begins to move objects about, and eventually his interest expands to include relations of objects to each other, as opposed to an exclusive concern with relations of objects to his actions with respect to them. This expansion is the beginning (but only the beginning) of a conception of *general space*.

Stage 4. Coordination of Secondary Schemata (8-12 months)

The title of the fourth stage is not very descriptive. Suffice it to say that in this stage there are refinements in each of the four categories that were used in analyzing Stage 3 (i.e., *Intention and Means-End Separation, Meaning, Incorporation of New Objects into Existing Schemata*, and *Object Permanence and the Construction of Space*). Beyond those, we shall need a new category of *causality*.

Intention and Means-End Relations

Here is another set of observations from *The Origins of Intelligence*. See what you make of it:

> [When he is six months of age] I present Laurent with a match box, extending my other hand laterally to make an obstacle to his prehension. Laurent tries to pass over my hand or to the side, but he does not attempt to displace it.... Same reactions at age six months, eight days; six months, ten days; six months, twenty-one days; . . . and seven months, ten days....
>
> Finally, at seven months, thirteen days, Laurent reacts quite differently. I present a box above my obstacle hand, but behind it, so that

he cannot reach the matches without setting the obstacle aside. After trying to take no notice of it, Laurent suddenly hits my obstacle hand as though to remove or lower it. I let him [lower the hand], and he grasps the box. I recommence to bar his passage, but I use as a screen a sufficiently supple cushion to keep the impress of the child's gestures. Laurent tries to reach the box, and, bothered by the obstacle, he at once strikes it, definitely lowering it until the way is clear.

With Laurent seven months and seventeen days old, I resume the experiment without there having been intervening attempts. First I present the object (my watch) 10 cm. behind the cushion (the object of course being visible). Laurent tries at first just to grasp the watch, then pauses to hit the cushion . . . . With Laurent age seven months twenty-eight days, instead of simply hitting the things that intercede between his hand and the object, Laurent applies himself to pushing them away or even to displacing them . . . . I present him a little bell 5 cm. behind the cushion. Laurent first strikes the cushion, as previously, but then depresses it with one hand while he grasps the object with the other. Same reaction with my hand. At age seven months, twenty-nine days, he immediately depresses the cushion with his left hand in order to reach the match box with his right. At eight months, one day, when my hand intervenes with the obstacle, I definitely feel that he depresses it and pushes harder and harder to overcome my resistance . . . At nine months, fifteen days, he pushes my hand away with his left hand while pulling at the object with his right . . . .[15]

No doubt the clearest impression that you received from these observations was that of *intention*—Laurent's dogged determination to reach the object despite the interposition of barriers to his actions.

But in the process of attaining his goal, he made use of a cleanly articulated subaction—that of removing the barrier. This represents a further development of the separation of *means* from *ends*. In fact, it is at this stage that the first unequivocal manifestation of that separation can be observed. The infant in the third stage had produced certain effects by responding in certain ways, like making things move by shaking the crib or by pushing the object. But that was only the beginning of intention and means-end separation. There, he lost interest if an obstacle were interposed between him and an object. In this stage, he attacks the obstacle. From these observations, it is clear that there is now a relatively clear separation of means from ends, and intention is a most compelling inference.

----

[15] *The Origins of Intelligence in Children*, 1952, pp. 216–219.

As will be shown later, the separation of means from ends has far-reaching implications. When the two are completely separated, so that the means becomes an end in itself, we have *play;* when they are differentiated but continually related, we have *problem-solving* behavior. Both originate in this primitive separation of means from ends.

Symbolic Meaning

You will recall that in Stage 3 the infant acknowledged the presence of an object by reinstating some bit of overt behavior that had previously occurred in its presence. Now, in Stage 4, something new has been added:

Observation 133:
At age nine months, sixteen days, Jacqueline ... likes the grape juice in a glass, but not the soup in a bowl. She watches her mother's activity. When the spoon comes out of the glass she opens her mouth wide, whereas when the spoon comes from the bowl, her mouth remains closed. Her mother tries to lead her to make a mistake by taking a spoon from the bowl and passing it by the glass before offering it to Jacqueline. But she is not fooled.... At age nine months, eighteen days, Jacqueline no longer needs to look at the spoon. She notes by the sound whether the spoonful comes from the glass or the bowl and obstinately closes her mouth [when it comes from the bowl]....[16]

When in Stage 3 the child recognized an object by reproducing an action that had previously occurred in its presence, I spoke of the action as the "meaning" of that object for the child. Now, the "actions" consist primarily of complex neural patterns that serve to "represent" the object.

Thus in place of the "motor meaning" of Stage 3, we have a "symbolic meaning" in Stage 4.

Incorporation of New Objects into Existing Schemata

Actions summarized by this title are so obvious that the category is included in our discussion mainly for reasons of symmetry—i.e., so

---

[16]*Ibid.*, p. 249. Another example: "At age eleven months, fifteen days, Jacqueline cries as soon as her mother puts her hat on."

that the discussion will parallel that of Stage 3. It is the nature of cognitive structures to apply themselves repeatedly to whatever parts of the environment that can be assimilated by them, and that process continues through the waking hours of every normal person on every day of his life.

Object Permanence and the Construction of Space

As already noted, the "reality" that surrounds us is a construction of the brain; moreover, the ability to make this construction is not given but acquired.

The following observation illustrates one of those acquisitions as it functions in Stage 4:

Observation 44:
[At nine months, seventeen days] Laurent is placed on a sofa between a coverlet *(A)* on the right and a wool garment *(B)* on the left. I place my watch under *A;* he gently raises the coverlet, perceives part of the object, uncovers it, and grasps it. The same thing happens a second and a third time. . . . I then place the watch under *B;* Laurent watches this maneuver attentively, but at the moment the watch has disappeared under *B,* he turns back toward *A* and searches for the object under that screen. I again place the watch under *B;* he again searches for it under *A* . . . .[17]

It is very interesting to note the similarity between this behavior and that of the famous McGill scotties. These animals had been raised to adulthood in small cubicles that deprived them of the varied experiences that normal dogs have while they are growing up; they had never even seen their keeper. Of the many tests administered to the dogs when they were removed from the cubicle,[18] the one depicted in Figure 2.2 seems especially similar to the Piaget "experiment" just quoted.

In the McGill experiment, a piece of food was placed at A, and the dog was carried to within a few inches of the food so as to be

---

[17] *The Construction of Reality in the Child,* translated by Margaret Cook, New York: Basic Books, Inc., 1954, p. 53. (Original French edition, 1937.)

[18] A narrated motion picture taken immediately after the dogs were released can be purchased directly from McGill University, Montreal, Canada. The same events are described in writing by W. R. Thomson and R. Melzack. "Early environment," *Scientific American,* vol. 194, no. 1 (January 1956), pp. 38–42.

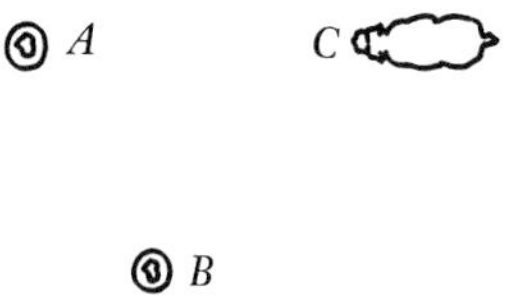

Figure 2.2

certain that he was attending to it. Then, with the dog watching from C, where he was being restrained by the experimenter, the food was moved to B. When the dog was released, he did not approach the place (B) to which the food had been moved, but trotted directly to the place (A) where he had originally seen it.

Don't the McGill experiment and Piaget's Observation 44 appear to be the same test with the same result? It is certainly an unexpected result, from a common-sense point of view; but from Piaget's point of view, and from Hebb's, it is just what should be expected. Later structures are built upon a foundation of earlier ones. In this, Piaget's fourth stage of the Sensorimotor Period, there is a shift in the child's conceptualization from object reality dependent on his own actions to object reality dependent on the surround.

The result is a kind of "context-bound object permanence." Or perhaps a more fitting inference—though it is not made explicitly by Piaget—is that this behavior represents instead an "overpermanence" of the object: it is still there to the child, even after it has been moved away. It is as though the central process representing the object is tied securely to others representing its immediate surround.[19]

The perception of space continues to develop during this period. Briefly, what happens is that the child becomes interested in objects as such rather than merely as aliments to his motor schemata, whereas new objects had previously arrested his attention only briefly before he did something with them. Now, he examines each object carefully in every possible way, as though it presented a problem to him.

One result is the ability to reverse the side of an object—e.g., earlier, when handed a bottle backward, the infant would make no effort to turn it around; now, he immediately reverses it so that the

---

[19] Even though I speak here of central processes that "represent" the object and its surround, Piaget does not acknowledge "true representation" until "no perceived sign commands belief in permanency." In this example, the screen is the "sign of the actual presence of the object"; thus we are not dealing here with a true representation (*The Construction of Reality in the Child*, 1954, p. 85).

nipple is toward him. It will be a long time before he can recognize what an object looks like from a different point of view, but this does seem to be a step in that direction.

Causality

It is in this fourth stage that we see for the first time clear indications of a construction that is anything like what an adult means by *causality*.

Previously, the infant was involved initially in every transaction that made any impression upon him; now, he can perceive objects other than himself as causes. The evidence for this is that he attacks barriers (as if they were "causing" his frustration) and that he sometimes waits for adults to do things for him (again indicating that there is a "cause" outside himself). There is a shift of interest from the action to its effect.

Stage 5. Tertiary Circular Reactions (12-18 months)

The Secondary Circular Reaction of Stage 3 was a consolidation of certain motor schemata by repetition of activities that produce interesting spectacles" that are integral parts of the activities themselves but which reinforce those activities. The Tertiary Circular Reaction[20] of Stage 5 is essentially the same process on a higher level: the "spectacle" is now separate from the overt action.

Intention and Means-End Separation

Here is a series of examples that illustrate the transition from secondary to tertiary reactions:

Observation 141:
This first example will make us understand the transition between secondary and "tertiary" reactions: that of the well-known behavior pattern by means of which the child explores distant space and constructs

---

[20] The reaction is called "tertiary" because instead of being concerned with actions of his own body, as in Primary Circular Reactions, or predominantly with the direct environmental consequences of these simple acts, as in Secondary Circular Reactions, the child now engages in "experiments" in order to discover new properties of objects and events.

his representation of movement: the behavior pattern of letting go of objects or of throwing them in order subsequently to pick them up.

One recalls (Obs. 140) how [at ten months, five days] Laurent discovered in "exploring" a case of soap, the possibility of throwing this object and letting it fall. What interested him at first was not the objective phenomenon of the fall, but the very act of letting go. He observed fortuitously, which still constitutes a "secondary" reaction, "derived," it is true, but of typical structure.

[At ten months, ten days, however] the reaction changes and becomes "tertiary." That day Laurent manipulates a small piece of bread (without any alimentary interest: he has never eaten any and has no thought of tasting it) and lets it go continually. He even breaks off fragments, which he lets drop. Now, in contradistinction to what has happened on the preceding days, he pays no attention to the act of letting go, whereas he watches with great interest the body in motion; in particular he looks at it for a long time when it has fallen, and picks it up when he can.

[At ten months, eleven days] Laurent is lying on his back but nevertheless resumes his experiments of the day before. He grasps in succession a celluloid swan, and box, etc., stretches out his arm and lets them fall. He distinctly varies the positions of the fall. Sometimes he stretches out his arm vertically, sometimes he holds it obliquely, in front of or behind his eyes, etc. When the object falls in a new position (for example, on his pillow), he lets it fall two or three times more on the same place, as though to study the spatial relation; then he modifies the situation. At a certain moment the swan falls near his mouth; now, he does not suck it (even though this object habitually serves this purpose), but drops it three times more while merely making the gesture of opening his mouth.

Observation 146:
[At one year, two months, eight days] Jacqueline holds in her hands an object which is new to her; a round, flat box, which she turns all over, shakes, rubs against the bassinet, etc. She lets it go and tries to pick it up. But she only succeeds in touching it with her index finger, without grasping it. She nevertheless makes an attempt and presses on the edge. The box then tilts up and falls again. Jacqueline, very much interested in this fortuitous result, immediately applies herself to studying it. Hitherto it is only a question of an attempt at assimilation analogous to that of Observations 136 and 137, and of the fortuitous discovery of a new result, but this discovery, instead of giving rise to a simple circular reaction, is at once extended to "experiments in order to see."

In effect, Jacqueline immediately rests the box on the ground and pushes it as far as possible (it is noteworthy that care is taken to push the box far away in order to reproduce the same conditions as in the first attempt, as though this were a necessary condition for obtaining the result). Afterward Jacqueline puts her finger on the box and presses it. But as she places her finger on the center of the box she simply displaces it and makes it slide instead of tilting it up. She amuses herself with this game and keeps it up (resumes it after intervals, etc.) for several minutes. Then, changing the point of contact, she finally again places her finger on the edge of the box, which tilts it up. She repeats this many times, varying the conditions, but keeping track of her discovery: now she only presses on the edge![21]

How do these adaptations differ from earlier ones? Doesn't the child indeed appear to be "experimenting" with new combinations of responses? And did you notice the continued slight variations as the pattern was repeated?

The "repetition of activities that produce interesting spectacles" is at a higher level here than in Stage 3, because instead of merely activating the pattern in a stereotyped manner, this child deliberately manipulates the environment to find out what happens, and continues to vary his approach even after an "interesting spectacle" has occurred. One is almost tempted to think of the Stage 5 baby as "the first scientist"!

Object Permanence, Space, and Time

Although the following quotation is very short, you may find in it evidence of advances in all three of the title categories. Try it and see.

Observation 54:
[At eleven months, twenty-two days] Laurent is seated between two cushions, *A* and *B*. I hide my watch alternately under each: Laurent constantly searches for the object where it has just disappeared—that is, sometimes under *A*, and sometimes under *B*, without remaining attached to the first, privileged position as during the fourth stage .... At twelve months and twenty days, he also searches sequentially in both my hands for a button I am hiding. Afterward he tries to see behind me when I make the button roll on the floor (on which I am seated), even though, to fool him, I hold out my two closed hands.[22]

---

[21] *The Origins of Intelligence in Children*, 1952, pp. 268–272.

[22] *The Construction of Reality in the Child*, 1954, p. 67.

Isn't it a reasonable inference that the object is now being represented by internal symbols? And did you notice the new independence of the object from its surround?

This new level of *object permanence* is a function of the subject's altered perception of space; and notice that a temporal sequence is also involved. There is internal representation of the object, and that representation has a unity and an independence not previously achieved. *Object permanence*, or the negation of "overpermanence" (p. 00); *space perception;* and *time perception* are all revealed at a higher level here than in the previous stage.

Subsequent observations indicate a limitation, however: these sequential displacements of an object can be followed only if the displacements are visible. If a toy is placed inside an open box and then the box is placed behind a screen and emptied there, the child will not think to look behind the screen for the toy when the empty box is handed to him.

Causality

By the time the child has reached Stage 5, his conception of *causality* has been further developed. He engages in some true imitation at this stage, and that has some implications for causality; but since I wish to treat imitation longitudinally after examining the other developments in the Sensorimotor Period, I shall not discuss it here.

Recall that in Stage 4 the child showed some appreciation of external causes by waiting for adults to serve him. Now, he not only waits, but actively solicits their help—to reach, push, open, etc.

The elaboration of means also has causative significance. When the child learns to use a stick or a string—e.g., to pull something toward him—he is constrained to *discriminate* between himself and the tool as the immediate cause of the movement of the object. That represents another step away from his original "the-world-is-my-actions-upon-it" conception of reality. His manipulation of objects begins at a higher level in this stage because of the means-end differentiation that has occurred in the previous one. In Stage 5 his behavior becomes even more purposive, as he continues to differentiate a variety of ends, and especially a variety of means.

The necessary culmination of this proliferation of means to a given end is a counter-trend in which ineffective means are discarded. An example is given on the following pages.

Observation 162:

[At fifteen months, twelve days] Jacqueline is seated in her playpen whose four sides are formed by vertical bars connected at base and summit by horizontal bars. The bars are 6 cm apart. Outside the pen, parallel to the side where Jacqueline is, I place a stick 20 cm long, which takes up the distance of about three spaces between the bars. We shall call these spaces, *a*, *b*, and *c*; space *b* corresponds to the middle part of the stick, and spaces *a* and *c* to the end parts. The problem is to transfer this stick from outside to inside the pen.

(1) Jacqueline begins by grasping the stick through space *b*. She raises it along the bars but holds it horizontally and parallel to the frame so that the harder she pulls the less it moves. She then extends her other hand through *c*, but holds the stick horizontally and does not succeed in making it come through. She finally lets go of the object which I put back in its initial position.

(2) Jacqueline begins over again by grasping the stick at *c*. In raising it, she tilts it up a little, by chance, and so makes it slightly oblique. She immediately takes advantage of what she perceives and, passing her hand through *c*, she tilts the stick until it is sufficiently vertical to pass through. She then brings it into the playpen through *b*. Why did she tilt it up? Was it through foresight or did she simply extend the movement, which was due to chance, so as to see what would happen?

(3–4) This time Jacqueline grasps the stick through space *c* at one of its ends. She draws it horizontally against the bars, but encountering resistance from them, she quickly makes it vertical and passes it through without difficulty. The speed of this adaptation is due to the fact that the stick was grasped by one of its ends.

(5) Jacqueline grasps the stick by the middle, at *b*. She raises it, puts it horizontally against the bars as in (1). She pulls and seems very surprised by a failure. It is only after a while that she tilts it and succeeds in bringing it in.

(6–10) Same reactions. At each new attempt, she begins by trying to make it penetrate horizontally parallel to the frame. Only after this initial failure does she tilt up the stick, still quite slowly.

(11) This time Jacqueline turns the stick more rapidly because she grasps it at *c*.

(12–15) She again grasps it at *b* and recommences to try to bring it through horizontally. Then she tilts it up, more slowly than at (11), and succeeds.

(16) She continues to take it at *b* and to try to pull it through horizontally, but this time she does not persist and tilts it up immediately.

(17) For the first time Jacqueline tilts the stick before it has touched the bar, and no longer tries to bring it in horizontally even though she grasped it at the middle.

(18–19) She begins by trying to bring it through horizontally, but it seems that this was due to automatism and she tilts it up immediately afterward.

(20 *et. seq.*) She finally turns it systematically before it touches the bars.[23]

Surely, but very slowly, the ineffective means drop out, until eventually the performance becomes deliberate and efficient. The process by which it becomes so certainly appears to be what Thorndike called "trial-and-error."[24] Piaget prefers "groping accommodation," because he says that the errors are not random responses, but rather that they are *inappropriate generalizations* of schemata that have been effective in other situations.[25] In any case, it is clear that in Stage 5 there has been a shift from stereotyped behavior to a kind of systematic variation of responses.

---

[23] *The Origins of Intelligence in Children,* 1952, pp. 305–306.

[24] Others have referred to it as "hypothesis testing"; I have not done so here because in Piaget's usage "hypotheses" do not appear until the Period of Formal Operations.

[25] When he repeated the bars problem with other objects (a book, a doll, a cardboard rooster) Piaget found, just as Harlow did later in his "learning-how-to-learn" experiments with monkeys, that his subject had to learn each solution from the beginning (in this case pulling the object against the bars) but that, also like Harlow's monkeys, she learned each solution more quickly than the last. Two other pertinent studies of nonhuman primates are those of Kohler and Birch (see Bibliography). Kohler had found very little of this "trial-and-error" in his chimpanzee subjects, but other psychologists later found that for subjects of the same species, working on the same problem that Kohler had given to his subjects (using a stick as an extension of the arm to rake in a distant piece of food), trial and error was the rule rather than the exception. Birch suspected that the critical difference might be related to the fact that his subjects were reared in the laboratory, whereas Kohler's animals had grown up in the jungle. He therefore arranged for several of his "failures" to have free play experiences with the sticks, then retested them afterwards. Every one of them solved the problem almost immediately, even though the sticks had not been used as rakes during the free-play period. Piaget would probably say that Birch's animals developed an extension-of-the-arm schema during the free play situation and then applied it effectively to the problem even though they had made no trial-and-error use of the sticks as rakes.

Stage 6. Invention of New Means Through Mental Combination (18-24 months)

The sixth and last stage of the Sensorimotor Period is, it seems to me, actually a transitional phase—transitional to the subsequent stage, the Preoperational Subperiod of the Concrete Operations Period. But I suppose that is what one should expect, since every unit in the series is transitional to the next.

Intention and Means-End Relations

The sixth stage is virtually defined by the important change that occurs in this category, Intention and Means-End Relations. It concerns the invention of new means through mental combinations. If one examines the entire Sensorimotor Period, one can discern three forms of intentionality and goal-directed behavior:

1. Applying familiar schemata to new situations (Stage 4).
2. Modifying familiar schemata to fit new situations (Stage 5).
3. Invention of new means through reciprocal assimilation of schemata (Stage 6).

The behavior of a child in this sixth stage is more like that of Kohler's jungle-reared chimps than that of Birch's laboratory-reared animals.[26] If the reader will recall my interpretation of the differences between the initial behavior patterns of these two groups of chimpanzees in the stick problem (Kohler's jungle-reared animals had had a richer "early experience" than Birch's), I think it will be relatively easy to interpret the differences Piaget reports between the way in which Laurent, on the one hand, and his sisters, on the other, acquired what Piaget calls "the pattern of the stick." The account is rather a long one, but its length is the very point of the illustration. See if you can tell why.

Observation 177:
In contrast to Jacqueline and Lucienne, who were submitted to numerous experiments during which they had opportunity to "learn" to use the stick, Laurent only manipulated it at long intervals until such time as he knew how to use it spontaneously. In order to characterize that

---

[26] What was tangential to the discussion on pages 33–35 is now central; read footnote 25 p. 35, again with the present context in mind.

moment, it is worthwhile to retrace briefly the ensemble of Laurent's earlier behavior patterns relating to the stick.

As early as four months and twenty days of age, i.e., at the beginning of the third stage, Laurent is confronted by a short stick, which he assimilates by shaking it, rubbing it against the wicker of his bassinet, etc. In general, he makes it the equivalent of the paper knife .... At four months and twenty-one days, when Laurent is holding the stick, he happens to strike a hanging toy and immediately continues.

But during the next hours, Laurent no longer tries to reproduce this result even when I put the stick back in his hand. This is not, then, an example of "the behavior pattern of the stick" .... The following days I give him the stick again and try to make him associate it to the activity of the various schemata, but Laurent does not react then or in the following weeks .... In the course of the fourth stage, characterized by the coordination of the schemata, he makes no progress in the use of the stick. During this stage, however, Laurent comes to use the hand of another person as an intermediate to act upon distant objects, thus succeeding in spatializing causality and preparing the way for experimental behavior. But when, at eight months or even nine months, I give Laurent the stick, he only uses it to strike around him and not to displace or to bring to him the objects he hits ....

[At twelve months], i.e., well into the fifth stage, when Jacqueline and Lucienne succeeded in "discovering" the utilization of the stick, Laurent manipulates a long wooden ruler for a long time, but arrives at only the three following reactions: (1) turning the stick over systematically while transferring it from one hand to the other, (2) striking the floor, his shoes and various objects with it, (3) displacing it by pushing it gently over the floor with his index finger. Several times I place at certain distances from Laurent some attractive object to see whether he, already holding the stick, will know how to use it. Each time, Laurent tries to attain the object with his free hand without having the idea of using the stick ....

[At fourteen months, twenty-five days] I give him back the stick because of his recent progress. He has learned to put objects on top of one another, to put them in a cup and turn it upside down, etc.: the relationships that belong to the level of the behavior of the stick .... Laurent grasps the stick and immediately strikes the floor with it, then strikes various objects placed on the floor. He displaces them gently, but it does not occur to him to utilize this result systematically .... I put various desirable objectives 50 cm or one meter away from Laurent, but he does not realize the virtue of the instrument he holds .... If I had repeated such experiments at this period, Laurent, like his sisters, would have discovered the use of the stick through groping and apprenticeship.

But I broke off the attempt and only resumed it during the sixth stage.

At sixteen months, five days, Laurent is seated before a table, and I place a bread crust in front of him, well out of reach. Also, to his right I place a stick about 25 cm long. At first Laurent tries to grasp the bread without paying any attention to the instrument, and then he gives up. I then put the stick between him and the bread; it does not touch the bread but nevertheless carries with it an undeniable visual suggestion. Laurent again looks at the bread, without moving, looks very briefly at the stick, then suddenly grasps it and directs it toward the bread. But he grasped it toward the middle, and not at one of its ends, so that it was too short to attain the objective. Laurent then puts it down and resumes stretching out his hand toward the bread. Then, without spending much time on this movement, he takes up the stick again, this time at one of its ends (chance or intention?), and draws the bread to him. He begins by simply touching it, as though contact of the stick with the objective were sufficient to see the latter in motion, but after one or two seconds at most he pushes the crust with real intention. He displaces it gently at first, but then draws it to him without difficulty. Two successive attempts yield the same results . . . . An hour later, I place a toy in front of Laurent (out of his reach) and a new stick next to him. He does not even try to catch the object with his hand; he immediately grasps the stick and draws the toy to him. Thus it may be seen how Laurent has discovered the use of the stick almost without any groping when, during the preceding stages, he handled it without understanding its usefulness. This reaction is therefore distinctly different from that of his sisters . . .[27]

The reader has undoubtedly noticed that there was in this illustration a gradual development followed by a sudden solution. But the gradual development is not *of* the solution: Birch's animals did not, during the stick play that followed their initial failure, use the sticks at all to rake objects toward them as required by the problem. What they learned was not a raking response, but a cognitive structure that could be applied to the new situation. The same was true of Laurent.

It is not, however, a cataclysmic change. There must have been some sudden change in the brains of Kohler's chimpanzees, and a similar change in Laurent; but Piaget would hold that it was not a basic restructuring, as Kohler believed. Rather, it was a new relationship among already existing elements. The elements themselves are changed in the process, but not drastically so.

Note that in what Kohler would have called an "insightful solu-

---

[27] *The Origins of Intelligence in Children*, 1952, pp. 33–36.

tion," the schemata function internally and are relatively independent of sensory input. In the words of Piaget, they do not require "a series of external acts to aliment them continually from without."[28] "The experimentation is interiorized, and coordination takes place before there is external adjustment."[29]

Object Permanence, Space, and Time

Laurent in Stage 5 had demonstrated object permanence by searching for an object in the place where it had just disappeared. But there the displacements had to be visible. Listen to this episode from Stage 6:

Observation 64:
[At age nineteen months, twenty days] Jacqueline watches me as I put a coin in my hand, then put my hand under a coverlet. I withdraw my hand closed; Jacqueline opens it, and then finding no coin, she searches under the coverlet till she finds the object.[30]

Piaget then repeats this test by hiding his hand in various other places before dropping the coin, and always with the same result. The child in Stage 5 is unable to follow the displacements of an object unless they are visible. Here, Jacqueline clearly is operating under no such handicap, for she now has "an actual image of the itinerary followed by the object . . . ."[31]

A less formal observation illustrates the same thing:

Observation 123:
At eighteen months, eight days, Jacqueline throws a ball under a sofa. Instead of bending down at once and searching for it on the floor, she looks at the place, realizes the ball must have crossed under the sofa, and sets out to go behind it. There is a table at her right, and the sofa is backed up against the bed on the left; therefore, she begins by turning her back on the place where the ball disappeared, goes around the

[28]*Ibid.*, p. 348. But even in the latter half of the Concrete Operations Period the child will be limited in the extent to which he can transcend direct experience. See pp. 100–101 of this book.

[29]*Play, Dreams and Imitation in Childhood*, translated by C. Gattegno and F. M. Hodgson, New York: W. W. Norton and Company, Inc., 1951. (Original French edition, 1945.) Again, it is not until the Formal Operations Period that the subject can deal effectively with "possibilities," as opposed to present realities.

[30]*The Construction of Reality in the Child*, 1954, p. 79.

[31]*Ibid.*, p. 82.

table, and finally arrives behind the sofa at the correct place. Thus, she has closed the circle of displacements by an itinerary different from that of the object . . . .[32]

What inferences can you draw from this concerning the child's conception of space? Perhaps many, but the major change indicated is the increasing importance of internalized symbols in the child's construction of space.[33]

Without going into detail, let me just say that the construction of time has undergone the same transformation as that of space: internal symbols make possible both memory of past events and anticipation of future ones. In Stage 6 the resulting temporal integration encompasses a considerable span.

Causality

This symbolizing has its effects in every one of the categories explored so far. Causality is no exception.

Observation 157:
[At eighteen months, eight days] Jacqueline sits on a bed beside her mother. I am at the foot of her bed on the side opposite Jacqueline, and she neither sees me nor knows that I am in the room. I brandish over the bed a cane to which a brush is attached at one end, and I swing the whole thing. Jacqueline is very much interested: she says "Cane, cane" and examines the swinging most attentively. At a certain moment, she stops looking at the end of the cane and obviously tries to understand. She tries to perceive the other end of the cane, and to do so, leans in front of her mother, and then behind her, until she has seen me. She expresses no surprise, as though she knew I was the cause.[34]

You can see from this illustration that it is now possible for the child to symbolize a *cause* by observing its *effect*. But what about vice versa?

---

[32] *Ibid.,* p. 205

[33] The quotation continues, ". . . and has thereby elaborated a group through representation by the invisible displacement of a ball and of the detour to be made in order to find it." The characteristics of a "group" are delineated on pp. 67 ff. The question of precisely what differentiates a Concrete Operations group from a Sensorimotor group is still being discussed among Piaget scholars.

[34] *Ibid.,* pp. 295–296.

Observation 160:

[At sixteen months, twelve days] Jacqueline has been wrested from a game she wants to continue and placed in her playpen, from which she wants to get out. She calls, but in vain. Then she clearly expresses a certain need, although the events of the last ten minutes prove that she no longer experiences it. No sooner has she left the playpen than she indicates the game she wishes to resume! Thus, we see how Jacqueline, knowing that a certain appeal would not free her from her confinement, has imagined a more efficacious means, foreseeing more or less clearly the sequence of actions that should result from it.[35]

Our subject apparently is capable not only of inferring cause from effect, but also of foreseeing the effect of a cause. Note that both of these are dependent upon the extension of time and space coordinates mentioned earlier; the effect of her action is projected in both. Thus it appears that the extension of time and space that occurs in this stage is accompanied by—and indeed is necessary to—a more sophisticated view of causality.

Imitation and Play—A Summary

Two categories of activity have so far been deliberately omitted from this analysis of the Sensorimotor Period. They are *imitation* and *play*. The reason for omitting them was not that they are in any way separate from other aspects of development, but rather that it seemed appropriate to close this account of the Sensorimotor Period with a longitudinal summary, and play and imitation lend themselves especially well to that purpose. Together, they can serve as a prototype of all development during that period.

You may recall that Piaget conceives of development as changes in structure through the action of invariant functions. There are just two of these functions,[36] *assimilation* and *accommodation*, and it happens that *imitation* is nearly pure accommodation and that *play* is

---

[35] *Ibid.*, p. 297.

[36] More precisely, he speaks of the invariant functions of *organization* and *adaptation*, with *assimilation* and *accommodation* as subcategories under the latter (see Figure 1.1).

almost entirely assimilation.[37] That is why a longitudinal treatment of these two is particularly instructive and can serve especially well as a review of the period.

Stage 1: Exercising the Sensorimotor Schemata (0-1 month)

Since behavior in this stage is essentially reflexive, there is nothing to say about imitation or play.

Stage 2: Primary Circular Reactions (1-4 months)

Imitation

In Stage 2 there are isolated instances of pseudoimitation: if someone else does something that the child has just done, the child repeats the pattern. That is not imitation; it is merely assimilation, into an already established schema, of the other's action as though it were his own.

Nevertheless, Piaget regards pseudoimitation as an intermediate stage in the development of true imitation.

Play

Once a primary circular reaction is mastered through combined assimilation and accommodation, it may become "autonomous," so to speak. Piaget cites the example of a Stage 2 child who has learned to throw his head back "to look at familiar things from this new position."[38] Having mastered this pattern, he begins to throw his head back without any apparent attention to what he can see by so doing.

When the accommodation becomes subordinated to the assimilation, the activity can be classified as play.

---

[37] You may object immediately that much children's play is imitative by its very nature ("playing cowboy," "playing house," etc.). But in these activities the imitative schema have already been mastered and are currently being assimilated into the play schema.

[36] *Play, Dreams and Imitation in Childhood*, 1951, p. 91.

Stage 3: Secondary Circular Reactions (4-8 months)

Imitation

In Stage 3 we find the beginnings of true imitation of sounds and movements that are already in the infant's repertoire. That is, he will often reproduce the actions of another even though he himself has not just previously been engaged in that action.

He reproduces only familiar patterns, however, and his actions still partake as much of assimilation as of accommodation. Moreover, the movements imitated must be visible on his own body.

Play

Although play remains essentially the same as in Stage 2, it is now easier to see the differentiation between play and adaptive assimilation.

An example of the change is the behavior of Lucienne, who discovered early on that she could make the objects hanging from the top of her cot swing. At three and one-half months, she studied this phenomenon seriously, "with an appearance of intense interest." At four months, however, "she never indulged in this activity ... without a show of great joy and power."[39] The serious work of comprehension, the accommodative aspect of the act, had dropped out entirely; what was left was pure assimilation — i.e., it was play.

Stage 4: Coordination of the Secondary Schemata (8-12 months)

Imitation

In Stage 3 the child could imitate only patterns that were already in his own repertoire and those that were visible on his own body. In Stage 4 he is relieved of both these limitations.

Because of the first-named limitation, the Stage 3 child's own actions and those of the model are relatively undifferentiated. Consequently, the imitation is not essentially different from the circular reaction, and the child continues the model's action as though it were his own.

---

[39] *Ibid.*, p. 92.

But in Stage 4, as subject and object begin to be differentiated, the child's view of the model's actions is quite different from what it had been previously. "Instead of appearing to be continuations of his own activity, they are now partially independent realities that are analogous to what he himself can do and yet distinct from it."[40] Once that change has occurred, the child develops an interest in novel actions and begins to imitate them.

I cannot help wondering whether the second of the two limitations of Stage 3 would ever be overcome if the child were deprived of the solicitous attention of adults whose imitations of his actions (facial expressions, pointing to various parts of the face, etc.) provide visual feedback correlated with kinesthetic and tactile inputs. I should think that a perpetually present mirror might serve that purpose even better.

Imitation of movements not visible on his own body cannot, like the earlier ones, be interpreted as direct assimilation of the model's behavior pattern into the child's established schema. Rather, it is accomplished by means of transitory "indices," such as a sound associated with a movement of the mouth. The index forms a kind of link—an element common to both patterns—between the visual input from the model and the tacto-kinesthetic input from the child's own movements. When a model says, "Ah," for example, and the child imitates him, the latter gets visual input from the model's open mouth and kinesthetic input from his own. But the child cannot match visual inputs from the two mouths, because he cannot see his own. His open mouth is "linked" to the model's by that which the two agents have in common: the auditory pattern, "Ah."

Play

The distinction between play and adaptive behavior becomes more clear in Stage 4 with the differentiation of means from ends. When the child pursues a means for its own sake he is obviously engaged in play. In the discussion of means-end relations in Stage 4, I referred to the child's attacking a barrier in order to reach a goal object that lay beyond it. When the same child later forgets all about the goal object in his zeal for attacking the barrier, the activity is clearly play.

The pattern called "ritualization" also begins during this stage, but a description of it is deferred until Stage 5.

---

[40] *Ibid.*, p. 50.

Stage 5: Tertiary Circular Reactions
(12-18 months)

Imitation

The change in Stage 5 is one of degree rather than kind. The child reproduces patterns of the model that are less similar to established schemata, and the reproduction is more precise than it was before.

Play

Stage 5 play is noteworthy for its elaboration of the "ritualization" that first appeared in the previous stage. Whereas Stage 4 rituals were confined to repeating and combining previously established adaptive schemata, in Stage 5 many patterns become games almost immediately, with no intermediate period of adaptive utility.

When Jacqueline's hand slipped from her hair and splashed into the bath water, she repeated the sequence with great glee, varying the heights, as she would if it were a tertiary circular reaction, but always grasping her hair first, which of course had no effect whatever on the ensuing splash.

On another occasion Jacqueline chanced to set an orange peel to rocking on a table immediately after having looked at its convex side, and that became a ritual. She rocked the orange peel at least twenty times, each time looking at its underside before proceeding further.

Stage 6: Invention of New Means Through
Mental Combinations (18-24 months)

Imitation

Stage 6 is marked by three advances over the previous one:

1. The child imitates complex new models without extensive trial and error.
2. He imitates nonhuman, even nonliving, objects.
3. He imitates absent objects.

Stage 5 was the era of overt experimentation, and the imitation that occurred there was overtly experimental. But now the experimentation is "interiorized," to use Piaget's term, and the pattern is worked out in his head before he ever does anything that the observer can see.

The imitation of nonhuman objects is important both because it serves the investigator as an indication that representation is going on, and because it can serve the child as the representation itself. When Jacqueline's doll got caught by its feet in the top of her dress, she extricated it, with difficulty; but as soon as she got it out, she tried to put it back again, apparently in an effort to understand what had happened. Failing in this, she crooked her forefinger into the shape of the doll's foot and placed it into the neck of her dress. After pulling briefly with the imprisoned finger, she removed it, apparently satisfied. Piaget interprets this as the construction of "a kind of active representation of the thing that had just happened and that she did not understand."[41]

This mechanism is reminiscent of the "motor meaning" of Stage 3. It is not the same, however, because that consisted merely of reactivating, in the presence of a particular object, the child's own movements that had previously occurred in the presence of that object, whereas the Stage 6 child reproduces the outline of an action of the object (in this example, the doll)—an act that the child has never before performed.

The final point about Stage 6 imitation is the main one: the child imitates models that are not physically present at the time of the first reproduction. This so-called "deferred imitation" is consistent with the previously discussed general intellectual characteristics of Stage 6 and is very important in the development of *play*.

Play

The distinctive characteristic of play in Stage 6 can be summed up in a single word: *symbolism*. What had previously been simple motor games are now representations of previous experiences; they are "make-believe."

Lucienne accidentally fell backward while sitting on her cot. Seeing a pillow, she seized it and pressed it against her face as though sleeping on it. Then after a moment she "sat up delightedly." This procedure was repeated many times during the day, even in places other than the cot and with no pillow available. Each time, she would first smile, and then throw herself back and press her hands against her face as though the pillow were there.[42] The symbolic basis of this behavior should be clear to any thoughtful observer.

---

[41] *Ibid.*, p. 65.

[42] *Ibid.*, pp. 96–97.

It is at this stage that play and imitation become fused, with the former dominating the latter. The progress of representational processes in general makes possible the "internal" or "deferred" imitation that is illustrated by the example cited above and that is an integral part of so much of the play (like the "playing cowboys" and "playing house" mentioned in footnote 37) that we see in older children.

A summary of developments in play and imitation, as well as in all other categories of the analysis, may be found in Table II.

Table II. Multidimensional View of Development During the Sensorimotor Period

Developmental Unit	Intention and Means-ends Relations	Meaning	Object Permanence
Exercising the Ready-made Sensorimotor Schemata (0–1 mo.)			
Primary Circular Reactions (1–4 mo.)		Different responses to different objects	
Secondary Circular Reactions (4–8 mo.)	Acts upon objects	"Motor meaning"	Brief single-modality search for absent object
Coordination of Secondary Schemata (8–12 mo.)	Attacks barrier to reach goal	Symbolic meaning	Prolonged, multi-modality search
Tertiary Circular Reactions (12–18 mo.)	"Experiments in order to see"; discovery of new means through "groping accommodation"	Elaboration through action and feedback	Follows sequential displacements if object in sight
Invention of New Means Through Mental Combinations (18–24 mo.)	Invention of new means through reciprocal assimilation of schemata	Further elaboration; symbols increasingly covert	Follows sequential displacement with object hidden; symbolic representation of object, mostly internal

pace	Time	Causality	Imitation	Play
			Pseudo-imitation begins	Apparent functional autonomy of some responses
ll modalities cus on ngle object	Brief search for absent object	Acts; then waits for effect to occur	Pseudo-imitation · quicker, more precise	More responses done for their own sake
urns bottle reach pple	Prolonged search for absent object	Attacks barrier to reach goal; waits for adults to serve him	True imitation —i.e., of novel response	Means often become ends; ritualization begins
ollows quential splacements object in ght	Follows sequential displacements if object in sight	Discovers new means; solicits help from adults	True imitation quicker, more precise	Quicker conversion of means to end; elaboration of ritualization
lves detour oblem; mbolic presentation spatial lationships, ostly internal	Both anticipation and memory	Infers causes from observing effects; predicts effects from observing causes	Imitates 1. complex, 2. nonhuman, 3. absent models	Treats inadequate stimuli as if adequate to imitate an enactment —i.e., symbolic ritualization or "pretending"

III

Concrete Operations Period
(2-11 years)

Preoperational subperiod (2–7 yr.) I: changes from
sensorimotor
> Essence of the change
> The symbolic function
> Adaptive behavior
>> Action-to-explanation
>> Scope
>> Summary
> Origins of the symbolic functions
>> Accommodation
>> Assimilation
> Relation to language

Preoperational subperiod (2–7 yr.) II: differences from
adult
> Concreteness
> Irreversibility
> Egocentrism
> Centering
> States vs. transformation
> Transductive reasoning

Concrete operations subperiod (7–11 yr.) I: introduction

Concrete operations subperiod (7–11 yr.) II: properties
of groups and groupings
> The group
> The lattice
> The grouping

III

Concrete Operations Period

In at least one place, Piaget has defined an "operation" as "an action that can return to its starting point, and that can be integrated with other actions also possessing this feature of reversibility."[1] But it seems clear from his actual use of the concept that an additional restriction should be included in the definition: the action is internalized. Flavell says that "any representational act that is an integral part of an organized network of related acts is an operation."[2] The reason for calling this new period "concrete operations" will become clear presently.

---

[1] Jean Piaget and Barbel Inhelder, *The Child's Conception of Space*, translated by F. J. Langdon and J. L. Lunzer, London: Routledge & Kegan Paul Ltd, 1956, p. 36. (Original French edition, 1948.)

[2] John H. Flavell, *The Developmental Psychology of Jean Piaget*, Princeton: D. Van Nostrand Co., Inc., 1963, p. 166.

Preoperational Subperiod (2-7 years)
I: Changes From Sensorimotor

Essence of the Change

The essential difference between a child in the Sensorimotor Period and one in the Preoperational Subperiod of Concrete Operations is that the former is relatively restricted to *direct interactions* with the environment, whereas the latter is capable of manipulating *symbols* that *represent* the environment. As was brought out earlier, the foundations of symbolic activity are laid during the Sensorimotor Period.[3] Moreover, it was shown that "motor meaning" develops in Stage 3, symbolic meaning in Stage 5, and in Stage 6 even the beginnings of symbol manipulation can be detected.

The "Symbolic Function"

But the Preoperational child has in his repertoire and can differentiate *signifiers* (words, images, etc.) from *significates* (those objects or events to which the words or images refer), whereas the Sensorimotor child apparently perceives the sign and its significate as a single unit— e.g., "tinkle-on-bowl-taste-of-soup" or "hat-on-mother-go-away," or even "pillow-thumb-sleep."

During the Sensorimotor Period you will remember that the infant did develop what we called "motor meaning," and that certain events then came to signify other events. But the point of making a division here is that the Sensorimotor child can seldom utilize any but concrete signals, whereas the Preoperational child can make an internal response —or a "mediating process," if you prefer—that represents an absent object or event. And he can differentiate the signifier (tinkle on bowl,

---

[3] Piaget is not consistent in his use of the term "symbol." In a single paragraph (*Play, Dreams and Imitation in Childhood*, p. 101) he says of the ritualizations of Stages 4 and 5 that "such actions are certainly not yet properly called symbolic, since the action is only a reproduction of itself and is therefore both signifier and signified," and then refers to those same rituals as "symbols" that serve as a preparation for the "representational symbols" that emerge later on. Perhaps the best recourse here is to place emphasis not on the change toward symbolic representations, but on the increasing differentiations of signifiers from significates; though again the issue is clouded, for Piaget sometimes includes the latter in his definition of the former (*Ibid.*, pp. 101–102).

hat on mother, pillow and thumb-sucking) from the significate (taste of soup, mother going away, going to sleep).

To summarize, then: entrance into the Preoperational Subperiod is marked by increasing internalization of symbols and increasing differentiation of signifiers from significates.

Adaptive Behavior

Intelligence might well be defined as the organization of adaptive behavior, and adaptive behavior is definitely different in the new period.

Action-to-Explanation

The Sensorimotor child is action-oriented; he is limited to the pursuit of concrete goals. The Preoperational child can reflect upon his own behavior—i.e., on the organization of his behavior as it relates to the goal rather than merely on the goal itself.

Scope

Whereas the Sensorimotor child is limited to linking successive perceptions of concrete objects and events through very *brief* anticipations of the future and memories of the past, the Preoperational child has access to a comprehensive representation of reality that can include past, present, and future and can occur in an exceedingly short period of time.[4] Piaget likens Sensorimotor intelligence to a motion picture both taken and projected very slowly so that "all the pictures are seen in succession, and so without the continuous vision necessary for understanding the whole."[5]

Summary

The eventual result of this extension in scope and of a shift of interest from action to explanation is the development of a system of codified symbols that can be manipulated and communicated to others.

---

[4] Hebb would probably speak here of the short-circuiting process whereby many of the "motor loops" drop out. Once this has occurred, we have what Piaget calls an "image."

[5] The official translation likens Sensorimotor intelligence to "a slow-motion film," but in a context that I believe clearly justifies my version. Piaget, Jean, *The Psychology of Intelligence*, translated by M. Piercy and D. E. Berlyne, London: Routledge and Kegan Paul Ltd., 1950, p. 121. (Original French edition, 1947.)

Origins of "The Symbolic Function"

Accommodation

"The symbolic function" has a great future; but what about its past? How did it get started? Probably the most important notion here is that of "internalized imitation." Just as absent events were "re-presented" in the Sensorimotor Period by overt imitations triggered by sensory input, so the representation is now accomplished covertly and without sensory aid by means of an imitation that has been made in the past and internalized. This, then, is the "signifier":[6] it signifies the event that was imitated; it can serve also as a kind of plan for future action.

As an example of this, do you remember Lucienne in the match box problem? When faced with a problem whose solution involved "opening," the opening plan was represented by the opening of her mouth.

That is a transitional case. Later on in the Preoperational Subperiod, the motor loops drop out, and the whole thing runs itself off without any perceptible movement.

Assimilation

All of what has just been said referred, of course, to accommodation. Where does assimilation fit in? Simply by being what it is: the process of signifying *is* essentially an assimilatory process—i.e., it is the process of supplying the significate when the signifier is evoked. Or, to put it another way, the signifier acquires meaning when it is assimilated to the schemata that represent the signified events.[7]

Actually, I have oversimplified this. Piaget classifies functions on the "representative" dimension as follows:

> *Accommodation*
> Effects of the present: simple accommodations.
> Effects of the past: representations and images.

---

[6] Two kinds of signifiers differ with respect to their referents:
1. "Signs": relation to significate is
   (a) arbitrarily selected,
   (b) socially agreed upon.
2. "Symbols": significate is
   (a) usually physically similar to signifier,
   (b) private, idiosyncratic.

[7] Again, the signifier is the imitation, the significate is that which is signified.

Assimilation

Effects of the present: incorporation of data into adequate schemata.

Effects of the past: connections established between the present schemata and "others whose meanings are merely evoked and not provoked by present perception."[8]

The added time dimension is a complication that causes difficulty in the equilibration of assimilation and accommodation, and this, in turn, causes the well-known instability of the period, in which the child is continually shifting among play, imitation, and intelligent adaptation.[9]

Relation to Language

Anyone who has ever thought about development has noticed the correlation of verbal ability with the general mental ability of "intelligence." But since correlations are not causes, we are left with the question of what causes what.

Nevertheless, many people have asserted, on the basis of the correlation, that "representational thought" results from the learning of words. Piaget does not agree with this view, for he points out that the first signifiers are not linguistic signs, but rather private symbols for which there are no signs.[10] Shaking his legs represents the bassinet fringe; laying down his head, grasping the blanket, and sucking the thumb represent going to sleep; opening and closing his mouth represents opening and closing a match box.

These are all *imitations*. When the imitations become internalized, Piaget calls them "images," and these images are the first true *signifiers*. (The significates are the complete objects or events being imitated.)

Identify, if you can, the signifiers and the significates in the following short observation.

Observation 77:
At twenty-one months Jacqueline saw a shell and said "cup." After saying this, she picked it up and pretended to drink. (She had often

---

[8] *Play, Dreams and Imitation in Childhood*, 1951, p. 241.

[9] One way of conceptualizing at least part of this instability is to think of the child as continually playing games, and that "reality is a game at which he is willing to play with adults and anyone else who believes in it" (*Play, Dreams and Imitation in Childhood*, 1951, p. 93).

[10] See footnote 6, p. 56, for the characteristics of signs and symbols.

pretended to drink with various objects, but in these instances the object was assimilated to the drinking schema. Here the identification of the shell with the cup preceded the action.) The next day, seeing the same shell, she said "glass," then "cup," then "hat," and finally "boat in the water." Three days later she took an empty box and moved it to and fro saying "motycar"....[11]

The signifiers are the child's internalized imitations of a shell or of a box. The significates are the broader sets of events in which these objects and their imitations have been embedded in the past—events that may themselves subsequently be acted out. The signifier process "shell" is assimilated into the schema of "cup" in one instance, of "hat" in another, and of "boat" in still another.

To put it another way, the meanings of the shell consist of the schemata to which it can be be assimilated. The words used by the subject in this example refer not to the conventional meaning of "shell," but to the idiosyncratic meanings that reside in this particular subject. Often the referent of a noun is not an object at all, but an action or class of actions. "Mommy" may refer to a large class of helping behaviors, and in certain contexts it means, "Help me!" Or the child may invent words to fit developed concepts—e.g., "It's raining and winding out." "Let me key the door," or "I can do it 'cause he teached me."

Apparently what the Preoperational child does is to assimilate words into his already established idiosyncratic symbol system.

Preoperational Subperiod (2-7 years)
II: Differences from Adult

We have been looking at the Preoperational Subperiod from a perspective gained by first studying the Sensorimotor Period. In short, we have compared this period with the one that preceded it. That is a defensible procedure, of course; but since we are all inclined to take our own intellectual processes for granted, it may be useful to point out ways in which the child's thought is still quite different from that of the adult.

I prefer to explore these limitations of Preoperational thought

---

[11] *Play, Dreams and Imitation in Childhood*, 1951, p. 124.

under six headings (even though Piaget himself has not done so, and there probably could be many more). The six are:

1. Concreteness
2. Irreversibility
3. Egocentrism
4. Centering
5. States versus transformations
6. Transductive reasoning

Inasmuch as Piaget coined these terms during the course of many years of research and writing, it should not be surprising to find much redundancy in any list of this length. In fact, that it is what we do find; in many ways his categories represent different ways of saying essentially the same thing.

Wordsworth expressed beautifully (as poets are wont to do) one point of view on the relation of language to thinking: "the word," he said, "is not the dress of thought, but its very incarnation."

Not so, says Piaget. Language is the vehicle by which thought is socialized and thus made logical, but it is not the original basis of, nor does it ever become the whole of, human thinking.[12] My analysis of intellectual development will therefore not be concerned exclusively with the development of language.

Concreteness

The reader may well have wondered why the name Concrete Operations has been given to the period dealt with in this chapter, especially since the ability to manipulate symbols is the main feature that differentiates this period from the one that preceded it. The answer is that compared to the Sensorimotor infant, the child who has reached the Concrete Operations Period is relatively flexible and abstract. But compared to an adolescent or adult, he is still very concrete-minded indeed.

Much of his thinking takes the form of what Piaget calls *mental experiment*. Instead of the adult pattern of analyzing and synthesizing, the Preoperational child simply runs through the symbols for events as the events themselves would occur if he were actually participating

---

[12] Cf. p. 129.

in them. This has implications for the next category in the list, the very important characteristic that Piaget calls "irreversibility."

Irreversibility

"Reversible" means "capable of being returned to its point of origin"; every mathematical or logical operation is reversible. For example:

> $3 + 5 = 8$, and
> $8 - 5 = 3$.

Or

> all men and all women = all adults, and
> all adults except women = all men.

You can

> add something to the "3" and then
> take it away.

You can

> increase the size of the group, and then
> decrease it again.

In each case, you have

> thought your way from one condition to another, and then returned to the starting point.

That is the defining characteristic of reversible thought. It is *not* a characteristic of the thought of a Preoperational child.

Note also that each of these changes is a part of a closed system in which any change in one part of the system requires compensating changes in some other part. For example:

> if $3 + 5 = 8$ and
> I increase the "3" by one,
> I must also decrease the "5" by the same amount if I am to stay within the system—i.e., the system of two numbers whose sum is "8."

It is of course not surprising that the Preoperational child cannot accomplish this reversal; after all, he hasn't yet been taught arithmetic.

But here is a problem that does not demand such special skill:

A four-year-old subject is asked:
    "Do you have a brother?" He says, "Yes."
    "What's his name?" "Jim."
    "Does Jim have a brother?" "No."[13]

That's a surprising answer, to say the least. Can you diagnose the difficulty?
    Perhaps Figure 3.1 will help.

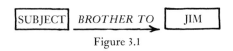

Figure 3.1

The relationship is one-way only; it is irreversible.
    Here is another astonishing illustration:

Two plasticene balls of equal size are prepared and shown to the child. He is asked,

      "Are they the same size, or
      does one have more plasticene in it than the other?"

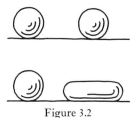

Figure 3.2

He says they are the same. Then—right before his very eyes—one of the balls is rolled into a sausage shape and he is asked the same question as before. This time he says that one has more plasticene than the other! Usually he says the sausage is the larger, but sometimes it is the ball.[14]

---

[13] From an observation of my own.

[41] Which it is depends on "centering." See p. 63, this volume, or Inhelder, "Criteria of Stages of Mental Development," *in* Tanner and Inhelder (eds.), *Discussions on Child Development*, New York: International Universities Press, 1960, pp. 75–85.

Why should a transformation performed entirely within his visual field and with his full attention produce such a result? The reason is that the child's thinking cannot reverse itself back to the point of origin. He does not "see" that since nothing has been either added or removed, the sausage could be made back into the original ball.

Another example very similar to the plasticene problem consists of comparing two equal amounts of liquid or two equal numbers of wooden beads in containers of different shape. Let us assume that beads are used.[15]

The child is given a pile of beads; he is then asked to pick up one in each hand.

> to put the one in the left hand into Container *A*,
> to put the one in the right hand into Container *B*, and
> to continue until there are no more pairs to pick up.

But Containers *A* and *B* are differently shaped, as shown in Figure 3.3.

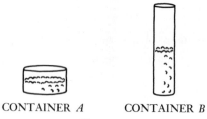

CONTAINER *A*   CONTAINER *B*

Figure 3.3

And when the subject is asked, "Which has the larger number of beads,

> Container *A* or
> Container *B;* or
> do they both contain the same amount?"

his answer is, "There are more in this one," and he points

> usually to *B*, but
> sometimes to *A*.[16]

The young child makes what to us are startling errors in thinking,

---

[15] This makes it a test of conservation of number rather than of quantity. I shall nevertheless refer henceforth to both of these problems (beads and liquid) together as "the water-level problem." See *The Child's Conception of Number*, 1952, pp. 25 ff.

[16] Which it is depends on "centering"; see p. 63.

even about simple transpositions that occur within his field of vision. He does so mainly because his thinking is *not reversible.*

Egocentrism

Just as the Sensorimotor child was "egocentric" in his overt actions, so the Preoperational child is egocentric in his *representations.*

The term "egocentric" is used, not in a pejorative sense, but descriptively to refer to his inability to take another person's point of view. He will speak to you using words that have idiosyncratic referents and using associations unrelated to any discernible logical structure; and then he'll be very much surprised when he fails to communicate. He is surprised because he cannot understand how you can see it any way but his way.

The ability to take the view of the other (without losing his own) and the corresponding social norm of logical consistency are acquired gradually, through repeated social interactions in which the child is compelled again and again to take account of the viewpoints of others. This social feedback is extremely important in developing the capacity to think about his own thinking, without which logic is impossible.[17]

Centering

Related to all the preceding characteristics is the one called "centering," or "centration." It refers to the child's tendency to center his attention on one detail of an event and, in fact, to his inability to shift his attention to other aspects of a situation. This inability is characteristic of the Preoperational child, and it has a disturbing effect on his thinking, as you may well imagine.

In the water-level problem, for example, he will center on either the height of the container (and say that the tall one is larger) or the width (and say that the wide one is larger). If it were possible for him to decenter in this problem, he could take into account both the height and the width, which would then allow him to relate the changes in one of these dimensions to compensatory changes in the other.

But the Preoperational child can not decenter, and—at least partly for this reason—cannot solve the problem.

---

[17] See also the sections entitled "Egocentricity in Representation of Objects" and "Egocentricity in Social Relations," pp. 83–84.

States versus Transformations

Also related to deployment of attention is the Preoperational child's tendency to focus on the successive *states* of a display rather than on the *transformations* by which one state is changed into another. Looking at the water-level problem with this tendency in mind, it is easy to see how it might hinder the child's thinking. After all, it is the transformation itself that would give an adult the feeling of certainty that the water poured from one beaker to another is the same water. It is as though the child were viewing a series of still pictures instead of the movie that the adult sees.

A dramatic illustration of this comes from an experiment in which the subject's task was "to depict (by actual drawings or by multiple-choice selection of drawings) the successive movements of a bar that falls from a vertical, upright position to a horizontal one."[18] A correct sequence would look something like that shown in Figure 3.4. That sequence is of course obvious to an adult, but the young child commonly fails to draw the intermediate positions of the stick—or even to recognize them when they are shown to him.

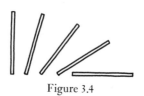

Figure 3.4

Preoperational children have much difficulty with this simple— and, to an adult, obvious—action sequence. They are unable to integrate a series of states or conditions into a coherent whole—namely, a *transformation*.

Transductive Reasoning

During the Sensorimotor Period we noted the gradual development of a conception of causality. Transitional between this and the reasoning of the adult is what Piaget calls "preconceptual" or "transductive" reasoning. Since Piaget is a logician as well as a psychologist,

---

[18] Reported by Piaget in *Bull. Psychol.*, Paris, 1959, and cited by Flavell in his *The Developmental Psychology of Jean Piaget*, 1963, p. 158. The words are Flavell's.

I prefer not to argue with him when he calls it "reasoning," but it certainly doesn't follow the familiar rules we know as reason. Instead of proceeding from the particular to the general (induction), or from the general to the particular (deduction), the Preoperational child proceeds from particular to particular (transductive reasoning).

The result is sometimes a correct conclusion, as it was when Jacqueline, at thirty months, twenty-seven days said:

"Daddy's getting hot water, so he's going to shave."[19] But sometimes it is rather strange:

Observation 111:
At two years, fourteen days, Jacqueline wanted a doll-dress that was upstairs: she said *"Dress,"* and when her mother refused to get it, "Daddy get dress." As I also refused, she wanted to go herself "To mommy's room." After several repetitions of this she was told that it was too cold there. There was a long silence, and then: "Not too cold." [I asked] "Where?" "In the room." "Why isn't it too cold?" "Get dress."[20]

The reader may object that this is merely common childish insistence on getting what he wants. That may be true, but it is just this common childish behavior that Piaget is trying to explain—or at least to classify. The fact is that childish insistence is qualitatively different from adult insistence.

In one of the above examples, the child's so-called "reasoning" led to a correct conclusion; in the other, it did not. But in either case, the same plan was followed, namely:

> *A* causes *B*, therefore
> *B* causes *A*.

"Daddy's shave requires hot water" is not different from
"Hot water requires Daddy's shave."

"A warm room makes possible the fetching of a dress" is not different from
"The fetching of the dress makes the room warm."

Another, somewhat different, pattern that is also called "transductive reasoning" concerns the child's lack of a hierarchy of categories.

---

[19] *Play, Dreams and Imitation in Childhood*, 1951, pp. 230–231.

[20] *Ibid.*, pp. 230–231.

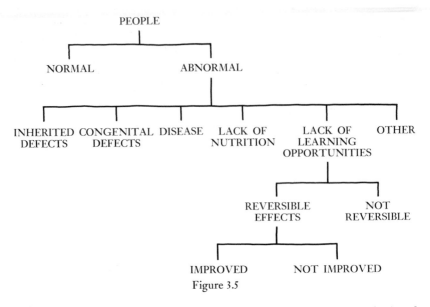

Figure 3.5

Adults can comprehend, for example, a hierarchy like the one depicted in Figure 3.5.[21]

But here is Jacqueline, dealing with a similar hierarchy:

Observation 112:
At twenty-five months, thirteen days, Jacqueline wanted to see a little hunchbacked neighbor whom she used to meet on her walks. A few days earlier she had asked why he had a hump, and after I had explained she said: "Poor boy, he's ill, he has a hump." The day before, Jacqueline had also wanted to go and see him, but he had influenza, which Jacqueline called being "ill in bed." We started out for our walk and on the way Jacqueline said: "Is he still ill in bed?" "No. I saw him this morning, he isn't in bed now." "He hasn't a big hump now!"[22]

Figure 3.6 shows the hierarchical pattern that must be built up in a person's mind before he can deal effectively with this type of problem. Jacqueline blithely transfers "recovery" in *A* to recovery in *B*, because her thinking lacks this heirarchical structure.

---

[21]Some Formal Operations adults fumble this one badly—e.g., when they categorize as genetically inferior a minority whose members have lacked learning opportunities. But Formal Operations adults are intellectually capable of doing better than that.

[22]*Play, Dreams and Imitation in Childhood*, 1951, p. 231.

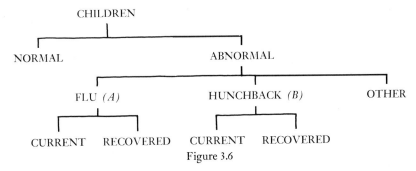

Figure 3.6

The reasoning is by simile:

A is like *B* in some way; therefore
A is like *B* in every way.[23]

It represents a kind of coarseness and rigidity—a lack of refinement and mobility—in the child's thinking. The child's limited hierarchical pattern includes only the normal and abnormal ("ill"), and individuals who are in one of those categories share all of its attributes.

Concrete Operations Subperiod (7-11 years)
I: Introduction

Having analyzed the Preoperational Subperiod in terms of the kinds of cognitive processes that differentiate it from the developmental units that precede and follow it, let us now do the same thing for the Concrete Operations Subperiod, but by comparing it with other periods in each of several different kinds of problems:

Conservation of numerical correspondence
Conservation of quantity, weight, and volume
Composition of classes
Numbering
Egocentricity in representation of objects
Egocentricity in social relations
Estimating water lines
Time, movement, and velocity

---

[23] Again, this is a fairly accurate picture of the rigidity that can be found in the thinking of many adults in certain situations (e.g., *A* and *B* both have dark skins; *B* is shiftless and irresponsible; therefore, so is *A*). Piaget does not deal with the question of why adult structures are not always used.

The various qualities of thought that I have discussed, and some that I have not, will manifest themselves in the solutions to these problems.

Before beginning, however, it might be useful to provide an additional framework for this discussion by pointing out that with the Concrete Operations Subperiod, Piaget's emphasis shifts to examining the relations between thinking and symbolic logic, and by sketching briefly the properties of the "groupings" of "concrete operations" that characterize this period of development. The rules of mathematics and logic are widely used by psychologists to govern their own behavior as scientists, but Piaget, in addition to this, uses them as models of the mental functioning of children. He is convinced that the rules of logic have developed out of the interaction of humans, both philogenetically and ontogenetically, with the exigencies of living in a lawful universe. The actions that we originally overt, and then internalized, now begin to form tightly organized systems of actions. Any internal act that forms an integral part of one of these systems Piaget calls an "operation." "Preoperational," "concrete operational," and "formal operational" describe different levels of systematic mental activity.

The actions implied by the mathematical symbols listed below are all examples of operations.[24]

$+$ combining

$-$ separating

$\times$ repeating

$\div$ dividing

$>$ placing in order

$=$ possible substitution

These have their counterparts in logic: e.g., "and" represents the action of *combining;* "except" represents the action of *separating.* Thus the structures of logic may be used to represent the structures of thought; the one serves as a model of the other.

This does not mean that people always think this way, but Piaget believes that any subject who ever thinks this way has a cognitive structure that can be represented in logical terms, and he describes other kinds of thinking as a failure either to use this developed structure or to develop the structure in the first place.

---

[24] Flavell, *The Developmental Psychology of Jean Piaget,* 1963, p. 166.

Concrete Operations Subperiod (7-11 years)
II: Properties of Groups and Groupings

In the Subperiod of Concrete Operations, structures often take the form that Piaget calls "groupings." A grouping combines the attributes of both the *group* and the *lattice*.[25]

The Group

A group is a system that consists of a set of elements and an operation on these elements such that the following principles apply:

Composition:[26] The result of every operation (remember that an operation is an action that is part of a system of actions) is itself a part of the system.[27] For example, if

$$A \times B = C,$$

C is a part of the system as well as A and B.

Associativity: When the operation is performed within the system,

$A \times (B \times C)$ is the same as
$(A \times B) \times C;$

combining A with the result of combining B and C is the same as combining C with the result of combining A and B.

Identity: In every system there is one and only one element that, when combined with other elements in the system, leaves the result unchanged. It is called the *identity element*.

$A \times I = A,$ and
$I \times A = A,$

where I is the identity element.

---

25 This discussion leans heavily on the synthesizing work of John H. Flavell in his *The Developmental Psychology of Jean Piaget*, 1963.

26 Sometimes called "closure," sometimes "combinativity."

27 The symbol $\times$ here stands for any operation on the elements A and B. Addition and multiplication of integers are examples.

For example,

> if the operation were multiplication, "*I*" would be 1;
> if it were addition, "*I*" would be 0.

Reversibility: For every element there is another that negates it. The negating element, called an *inverse*, is the only one that, when combined with the first element, yields the identity element.

$$A \times A' = I,$$

where A' is the inverse of A.

> If the operation were addition, the inverse would be $(-A)$;
> if it were multiplication, the inverse would be be $(1/A)$.

Here is a set of *elements:*

> 1   2   3   4   5   6   7   8   9

Let us say that the operation is addition. Is this set a group? The way to find out is to check it against the four properties described above, namely:

> *Composition:* The product (sum) of 8 and 9, for example, is 17, which is not within the system.
> *Associativity:* $(2+4)+(6+8) = 2+(4+6)+8 = 2+4+(6+8)$, or any other example you may choose.
> *Identity:* There is no identity element in the set.
> *Reversibility:* There is no inverse.

The set meets only one of the criteria; it is not a group unless it meets all four.[28] What if the set were changed to include all positive and negative integers plus zero?

> *Composition:* The sum of any two or more integers yields an integer. $3+5+9 = 17$.
> *Associativity:* It matters not whether the sum of 3 and 5 is added to 9 or 3 is added to the sum of 5 and 9.
> *Identity:* Adding zero doesn't change anything.
> *Reversibility:* For each positive integer there is a negative that cancels it. $3+(-3) = 0$.

This one does have all the properties of a group.[29]

---

[28] It is a lattice, however. See pp. 71 ff.

[29] And also of a lattice.

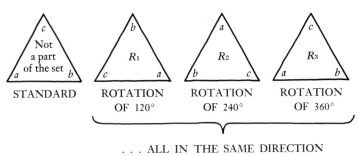

. . . ALL IN THE SAME DIRECTION
Figure 3.7

Figure 3.7 shows a set of three spatial elements; the operation is "followed by." This can be analyzed in the same manner as the sets mentioned above, by checking for the four properties of the group:

Composition: The product of any two or more of these rotations is also one of them.

$$R_1 \times R_1 = R_2,$$
$$R_1 \times R_2 = R_3,$$
$$R_1 \times R_3 = R_1.$$

Associativity: Given a specific set of rotations, it does not matter in what combination the operations are performed.

$$(R_2 \times R_2) \times R_1 = R_1 \times R_1 = R_2,$$
$$R_2 \times (R_2 \times R_1) = R_2 \times R_3 = R_2.$$

Identity: Because R_3 returns to its point of origin, it is the identity element in the set.

Reversibility: R_1 is the inverse of R_2 and vice versa, because their product is R_3, the identity element.

The set meets all the requirements of a group.

Thus not all systems of elements joined by a single operation are groups. Those that are have all four of the prescribed properties in common.

The Lattice

A lattice is a structure consisting of a set of elements and a relation that can encompass two or more of these elements. Specifically, this relation must be such that any two elements have one *least upper bound* (l.u.b.)[30] and one *greatest lower bound* (g.l.b.).[31] The least upper bound of two elements is the smallest element that includes them both. If element *B* includes element *A*, then the l.u.b. of *A* and *B* is *B*. In a hierarchy of classes, for example, if Class *B* includes *A* as a subclass, the l.u.b. of *A* and *B* is *B* (see Fig. 3.8). Similarly, the greatest

Figure 3.8

lower bound is the largest element that is included in both. Since *A* is included in *B*, but *B* is included only in itself, the g.l.b. of *A* and *B* is *A*.

Here is a set of elements:

1   2   3   4   5   6   7   8   9

Again, the operation is addition. Is the set a lattice? Take 5 and 9, for example:

9 is the smallest element that includes both (l.u.b.) and
5 is the largest element that is included in both (g.l.b.).

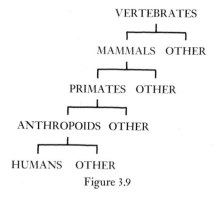

Figure 3.9

Figure 3.9 shows another set of elements, this one arranged in a class hierarchy. Can you find an l.u.b. and a g.l.b. for any pair of these elements?

---

[30] Sometimes called the "join."

[31] Sometimes called the "meet."

Take the pair "vertebrate-mammal," for example:

> *Vertebrate* is the smallest class that includes both classes, and *mammal* is the largest class that is included in both.

Other possible two-element relations are: mammal-primate, primate-anthropoid, and anthropoid-human. Since in any one of these it is possible to find both an l.u.b. and a g.l.b., this hierarchy is therefore a lattice. As a matter of fact, the lattice seems to be a particularly useful device for representing logical classes and relations in hierarchical form.[32]

The Grouping

We have now had a brief look at the properties of *groups* and of *lattices*. *Groupings* include them both. Nine distinct groupings make their appearance during the Concrete Operations Subperiod. Describing them all would be beyond the scope of this book, but fortunately the first one ("Grouping I") illustrates the basic characteristics of all of them (see Fig. 3.10). Grouping I, Primary Addition of Classes, is

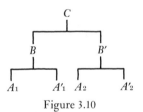

Figure 3.10

concerned with class hierarchies of the form $A + A' = B$, $B + B' = C$, etc., where A is an independently defined category and A' comprises "all the B that is not A." For example, if A were "human" and B were "anthropoid," A' would be "chimpanzee, gibbon, gorilla, and orangutan." The *posing*[33] of a class is logical *addition;* its *unposing*[34]

---

[32] Piaget himself uses the classes-and-relations structure to illustrate the properties of a lattice. It might better be called a "semilattice," however; because although all the vertical relations in the diagrams *(A, B,* and *C,* etc.) meet the requirements of a lattice, the horizontal ones *(A* and *A', B* and *B', C* and *C',* etc.) do not. The members of a horizontal pair are exclusive classes by definition.

[33] "Setting up" or "thinking of."

[34] "Excluding" or "omitting."

is *subtraction*. The nature of the hierarchy becomes apparent when we add two subordinate classes:

> Posing both A and A' is the equivalent of posing B;

> Posing B and B' together is the same as posing C.

Conversely,

> $B - A = A'$, and
> $B - A - A' = 0$.

Using the notation just presented, turn back to Figure 3.9 and note that if the class "humans" were designated as A, then "anthropoid" would be B, "primates" C, "mammals" D, and "vertebrates" E.

Now try translating the equations given on pages 73 and 74 into the more concrete terms of the zoological classification:

> $A + A' = B$ becomes, for example,
> humans + anthropoid apes = all anthropoids;

> $B + B' = C$ is now
> anthropoids + monkeys, lemurs, etc. = all primates;

> $B - A = A'$ becomes
> anthropoids – humans = anthropoid apes;

> $(B - A) - A' = 0$ is now
> anthropoids – humans – anthropoid apes = an empty or null class.

These are but a few of the many examples that could be given; many more could be generated by the single hierarchy depicted in Figure 3.9. They would all have characteristics of both group and lattice,[35] but Piaget believed that children's behavior was consonant with neither the group nor the lattice as such; so he formulated a hybrid, the grouping, as a more adequate model of this stage of their thinking.

At this point I am constrained to make a comment that may either anger or relieve the reader, depending on how meticulously he has

---

[35] But not all of those characteristics. When this class hierarchy was presented as a lattice (p. 72), I pointed out that it did not have all the properties thereof. The same must be said of it as a group, for $B-A-A'$ lacks associativity; $(B-A)-A' = 0$, but does $B-(A-A')$? Actually, A' cannot be subtracted from A at all, because the two are exclusive categories.

worked to master the material so far presented. My comment is this:
It is not the details of the system presented here that are important;
what is important is *the idea of system itself*. Piaget does not conceive
of responses being connected to stimuli as the child develops, but
rather of actions being related to other actions within a *system* of
actions. Any change in one part of that system has implications for
other parts.

Concrete Operations Subperiod (7-11 years) III: Some Representative Problems

With the properties of groupings in mind, let us proceed to analyze as best we can the behavior of children who are faced with the
various kinds of problems that were mentioned in the introduction to
this Subperiod:

Conservation of Number

One of these problems was devised as a test of an ability called
Conservation of numerical correspondence. The subject is presented
with several vases arranged in a neat row and a larger number of
flowers in a bunch. He is asked to arrange the flowers "one flower for
each vase, as many vases as flowers."[36]

Preoperational

Early in the Preoperational Period, the child cannot even arrange
the flowers in a one-to-one relation with the vases. He may set up
two lines of equal length, and then be surprised if they don't come
out even when he actually places the flowers into the vases.

Later, when he is able to establish the one-to-one correspondence
by himself, he can easily be fooled if the experimenter arranges one
set of objects (the vases) in a line and the other set (the flowers) in
a cluster, in which case he perceives it to be no longer equal to that

---

[36]Jean Piaget and Alina Szeminska, *The Child's Conception of Number*, translated by C. Gattegno and F. M. Hodgson, New York: Humanities Press, 1952,
p. 49. (Original French edition, 1941.)

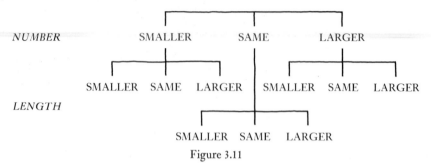

Figure 3.11

of the vases, even if each flower is taken directly from a vase just prior to the rearrangement.

In terms of the "limitations of the Preoperational child" listed on page 59, this performance would seem to involve at least *centering, states vs. transformation, irreversibility,* and *transductive reasoning.* And all of these can be conceived in terms of class-and-relations structure (see Fig. 3.11). The row of flowers can be classified as smaller than, the same as, or larger than the row of vases. But this can be done in either of two dimensions, number or length. Apparently what happens is that the subject fastens upon the length dimension of the row of flowers *(centering, states vs. transformation)* and fails to return to the representation of "same number" *(irreversibility, transductive reasoning.)*

The child of this age lacks the classes-and-relations structure; and until he has that, these "limitations" will recur.

Concrete Operations

In the Concrete Operations Subperiod, however, there is never any question about the outcome. The child not only arranges the display correctly, but is certain that he is correct; and he cannot be fooled when the experimenter arranges one of the sets into a cluster. When asked why he answers as he does, he says something like "They came out of the vases, so they'll go back into them." The *decentering* and *reversal* processes are effective, and the equivalence of the sets is permanent.

Conservation of Quantity, Weight, and Volume

Very similar kinds of problems are used to assess conservation of quantity, weight, and volume. The meaning of the term "quantity" in common speech is clear only in context; the same is true here. In these

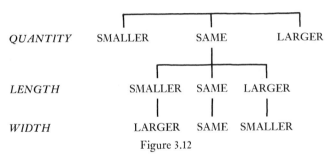

Figure 3.12

problems, when the word "quantity"[37] is used, it refers to the *amount of space* occupied by the object when the child is looking at the object and only at the object; but when that same occupied space is inferred from amount of water displaced by the object, it is called "volume." "Weight" is what might be expected—namely, the effect that the object has on the movement of a balance. The molded plasticene problem cited earlier (p. 61) can be used as an example of conservation of quantity; let us first review the reaction of the Preoperational child to that problem and then compare it with that of the child in the Concrete Operations Subperiod.

Preoperational

The Preoperational child cannot conserve at all. If the experimenter rolls the ball into a sausage right before the subject's eyes, the child will say that it is larger (or sometimes smaller) than the comparison ball. Refer to the list of limitations on page 59 for the reasons. Again *centering, states vs. transformation, irreversibility,* and *transductive reasoning* seem especially appropriate.[38] And again all of these limitations may be conceived in terms of a lack of mobility within a classes-and-relations structure.

The "sausage" can be classified as smaller than, the same as, or greater than the ball. But this classification can be done on at least three bases: quantity, length, and width. (Depth, an obvious fourth one, will be omitted for the sake of simplicity.)

Figure 3.12 shows these relations. Remember that it represents a

---

[37] Sometimes called "substance."

[38] One very important characteristic of the conservational structure was not stressed in the early writings and is not a part of the list on p. 59. Notice in Figure 3.12 that the third-order classification (width) is not a mere duplicate of the first and second (quantity and length); its freedom is restricted. If the quantity is the same (the special condition of conservation) and the length is smaller, the width cannot be "smaller, same or larger"; it can only be larger. Similarly, if the length is larger, the width can only be smaller. The usual term for this special feature of conservation is "compensation."

structure that the Preoperational child has not yet developed. He cannot move easily from one to another part of the figure in accordance with the rules implicit in it (always follow the lines). Instead, he centers on the length (or width) dimension and on the end state rather than the transformation—an end-state that he blithely transfers from one dimension to another. Furthermore, he is committed to that end-state; he cannot mentally reverse the transformation and arrive back at "same quantity."

It is tempting to think of *reversibility* as analogous to Hebb's "autonomy of central processes." Without this autonomy, children are dominated by their perceptions.

Perceptual domination can be demonstrated even in adults under special conditions. Such conditions do, in fact, obtain in Figure 3.13. The best way of demonstrating this is to administer to yourself the following brief psychomotor test:

> Place the butt end of a pencil or a pen within the alley at the very top of Figure 3-13. Your object is to reach the center of the spiral as quickly as possible without leaving that alley. Now look at your watch, note carefully what the time will be at the next even minute, and then, at exactly the time you have noted, begin.

Figure 3.13

How long did it take? Did you finish? If not, then you are now in a position to *think* of this figure as a series of concentric circles instead of a spiral. Having taken the prescribed "test" your thinking is no longer dominated by your perception; but you still can *perceive* it in only one way.

The Preoperational child is as unable to process information from the molded plasticene as "same quantity" as you were initially unable to process information from Figure 3.13 as "concentric circles." In both child and adult, *perception* is the dominant mental activity. The difference between them is that when you discovered that the path did not lead to the center, you *could* conceptualize the figure in those terms; that is, your mental processes exhibited mobility within a conceptual structure. The Preoperational child cannot; his thinking lacks that mobility.

Concrete Operations

When he can do it, he has moved into the Concrete Operations Subperiod. At about the age of seven, he conserves *quantity* but denies that the *weight* remains the same when a plasticene ball is molded into a sausage. Later (at around nine years of age), he conserves *weight* but not volume.[39]

Composition of Classes

Part-to-part and part-to-whole relations have been studied by Piaget under the heading Composition of Classes. The materials he used in one study[40] consist of three cardboard boxes and 20 wooden beads (18 brown ones and 2 white ones). All of the beads are spread out, clearly visible, on the bottom of one of the boxes.

---

[39] It is not until he enters the Period of Formal Operations, at around eleven or twelve years of age, that he is able to conserve volume. That is, if you immerse that now-familiar plasticene pair, the ball and the sausage, in equal amounts of water held in twin beakers, he can tell by the level of the water that the two immersed objects are equal. This achievement apparently awaits the development of an integrated system of spatial coordinates such that a part of a given volume can be "used up" by an object, so that any material that had previously occupied that space must be displaced by an amount equal to the volume of the object. This requires a somewhat more complicated cognitive structure than seeing a piece of plasticene as the same size when it is altered in shape.

[40] *The Child's Conception of Number*, 1952, p. 165. The "quotations" are actually paraphrasings of the original.

Preoperational

Here is what happens if the child is in the early part of the Pre-operational Subperiod:

> E: If I take the brown beads out and put them here into an empty box will there be any beads left in this one (the original box)?
>
> S: Yes, the white ones.
>
> E: If I take out the wooden beads and put them here (second empty box) will there be any left in this box (the original box)?
>
> S: No.
>
> E: Which would make the longer necklace, the brown beads or the wooden ones?
>
> S: The brown ones.

This surely is a surprising response, from an adult point of view. It is surprising because adult thinking depends upon structures that the Preoperational child does not have. In this case, an adequate structure might be something like that depicted in Figure 3.14.

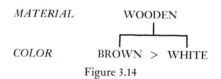

Figure 3.14

According to the principle of composition, the class of wooden beads is part of the system that includes the brown ones and the white ones, but for the Preoperational child that is not so. His approach to the problem is characterized by *centering* (on the color dimension), *irreversibility* (from the parts back to the whole whence they came), and *transductive reasoning* (a part-to-part relation that excludes the part-to-whole relation).

Concrete Operations

By the time the child is 7 years old, he will answer firmly that the wooden beads necklace would be longer because "there are more wooden beads than brown ones."

Numbering

According to Piaget, numbering is a synthesis of two other operations: *classifying*, or "cardination," and *ordering*, or "ordination."

Cardination is the answering of the question, "How many?" As such, it partakes of the nature of classifying, in that all the objects within a class are treated as *equal*. But in order to ascertain the composition of the class "5," for example, one must arrange the objects in a *series*, and the members of a series cannot be equal (must be *ordered*). Numerical units are therefore all different from each other during an operation that results in the formation of a class of identical elements.

Furthermore, the child does not really understand numbering until he can synthesize these two into a single reversible operation. "Reversible" here means that he can move back and forth from cardination to ordination.

Let's see how these conceptions apply to Piaget's "dolls-and-sticks problem."[41] Here the child is presented with 10 dolls that differ greatly in height and 10 sticks that also vary in length, but less so than the dolls do. He is told that the dolls are going for a walk and is asked to arrange the dolls and sticks "so that each doll can easily find the stick that belongs to it."[42] If he succeeds in this, it will be by placing the two series parallel to each other, each in serial order of size, as indicated in Figure 3.15. But then the experimenter spreads the sticks apart, so that corresponding elements of the two series are no longer opposite

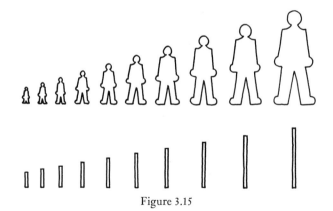

Figure 3.15

[41] *Ibid.*, pp. 97 ff.

[42] *Ibid.*, p. 97.

each other, points to one of the dolls, and asks, "Which stick will this one take?"[43]

Preoperational

In the early part of the Preoperational Subperiod, the child fails to make even the semblance of a correct response to this problem. He fails to match the two series because he cannot arrange either one by itself into the proper order; and he cannot arrange any series in order because he lacks the structure by virtue of which any two relations $A > B$ and $B > C$ may be joined into a superordinate relation $A > C.$[44] (See Fig. 3.16.) This property of "transitivity" is essential to any serializing operation, and without it, of course, the matching of sticks to dolls is impossible.

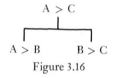

Figure 3.16

Later in the Preoperational Subperiod, the child can construct a series if given enough time, and he can match the sticks to the dolls if both are arranged in the same order; but if the two series are reversed —so that in one the units get bigger from left to right, but in the other from right to left—he fails again.

What he frequently does with the reversed series is to count; but when he "counts," all he is doing is pointing to one object after another while saying numbers that he has been taught to say in a given order. That is not true numbering, because the child has not yet achieved a synthesis of ordination and cardination.

Lacking that synthesis, the Preoperational child will often select the large (or small) end of each series as a starting point, mechanically count the dolls up to, but not including, the reference doll, and then count the same distance from the end of the series of sticks (see Fig. 3.17). His mental activity is probably something like this: he *classifies* three dolls as smaller than the reference doll (remember that the members of a class are all alike); then he counts the members of that class;

---

[43] *Ibid.*, p. 97.

[44] Without it, he has no compunctions about placing C before B in the series if he happens to be centering on the A-C relation at the time.

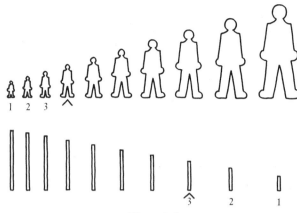

Figure 3.17

and finally he applies the resulting *cardinal* number to the stick series, with only a fleeting reference to order as he locates the starting point.

He can arrange the objects in order of size, but when he does so, he ignores their number; and he can count, but when he does so, he ignores differences in size.

Concrete Operations

It is not until he reaches the Concrete Operations Period that he is able to put these two operations together. Now he can select the matching stick for any specified doll, even though the series are reversed, because cardination and ordination are for him parts of a single system.

Egocentricity in the Representation of Objects

Even the Preoperational child has well-developed representational processes, as I have said; but there are still significant limitations on this ability. One such limitation is the inability to imagine an object from the perspective of another person.[45] Piaget and Inhelder[46] have devised a simple test of this, called the "three-mountain problem (see Figure 3.18).[47] They set three "mountains" on a table and one chair at each

---

[45] See also the sections on "Egocentrism," pp. 63 and 102.

[46] *The Child's Conception of Space*, 1956, p. 210.

[47] Adapted from Piaget and Inhelder, *The Child's Conception of Space*, 1956, p. 211.

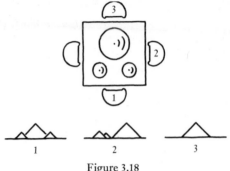

Figure 3.18

side of the table. The child sits in one of the chairs, and a doll is moved from one to another of the three remaining chairs. Then the subject is asked what the doll sees from each of its three stations. He may respond by drawing a doll's-eye view from each position, by selecting from drawings already made, or by constructing the doll's view with cardboard cut-outs.

Preoperational

The Preoperational child simply cannot do this at all.

Concrete Operations

In the early part of the Concrete Operations Subperiod, some transformations are correctly made, but performance is extremely erratic. It is only in the latter half of the Subperiod that the child can identify the doll's view with confidence and accuracy.

Egocentricity in Social Relations

Related to the child's ability to take another person's point of view toward a physical display are certain naturalistic observations of children in social situations—notably, situations in which they interact with each other.[48]

Preoperational

There is a strong tendency, in such situations, for children in the Preoperational Subperiod to engage either in *simple monologues*, which

---

[48] See also the sections on "Egocentrism," pp. 63 and 102.

conform to the content of their own individual activities, or in *collective monologues*, in which Child *A* says something to Child *B*, with no apparent intent that Child *B* should reply, or even hear; whereupon Child *B* does not, in fact, give any indication that he has heard, and responds by saying something totally unrelated to what Child *A* has just said.

They are incapable of intercommunication because neither of them is capable of taking the role of the other.

Concrete Operations

The development of concrete operations, with its increased mobility of thought, permits the child to shift rapidly back and forth between his own viewpoint and that of the other person.

It also makes possible the sharing of goals and the recognition of mutual responsibilities in the attainment of shared goals. In short, it makes cooperation possible.

And finally, it is at about this time (age seven) that children begin to be interested in games with rules. In order to play such a game, one must be able to conceptualize the roles of the other players, and in fact, children do develop this interest at the very same time that they begin to show in other ways their emancipation from egocentricity.[49]

Estimating Water Lines

Hebb suggests that even the simplest of object perceptions is built up of smaller elements that are themselves learned. It should not be surprising to find, then, that development of an extensive system of spatial coordinates takes even longer.

It shouldn't be, but it is! Here is the demonstration: a child is presented with a glass bottle one-fourth filled with colored water and another (or an outline drawing thereof) just like it but without the water. The second bottle is tipped off the vertical and the subject is asked to indicate where its waterline would be if the water from the first bottle were poured into it.[50]

---

[49] They find it difficult, however, to empathize with any younger child who spoils their game because he lacks this ability to conceptualize the interrelationship of roles.

[50] Drawings adapted from Piaget and Inhelder, *The Child's Conception of Space,* 1956, p. 383.

Preoperational

In the latter part of the Preoperational Subperiod, the child centers on the configuration of the bottle, and the waterline is drawn with reference to that only (Fig. 3.19).

Figure 3.19

Concrete Operations

The early part of the Concrete Operations Subperiod is a transitional stage in which there is a conflict between taking reference cues from the bottle and using the more stable horizontal and vertical con-

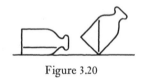

Figure 3.20

tours of the surround (Fig. 3.20). It is not until the child is nine or ten years old that he is able to give the correct response consistently (Fig. 3.21).

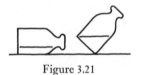

Figure 3.21

To me, the striking thing about all this is that the Euclidean space that we all take for granted not only is constructed rather than given, but is constructed over a period that covers most of a person's growing years.

Time, Movement, and Velocity

Another such construction is that of *time*.[51] Children's answers to questions about time are often mildly surprising to adults, but when observations are made in situations deliberately contrived to illuminate the salient features of their thinking, the results are sometimes down-right astonishing!

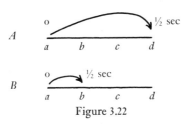

Figure 3.22

If the experimenter moves one object *(A)* from *a* to *d* and simul-taneously moves another object *(B)* from *a* to *b* (Fig. 3.22), the early Preoperational child will insist that *A* "took longer" than *B*. Even more

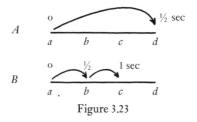

Figure 3.23

surprising is his response when the *B* object is moved twice (Fig. 3.23). The child may still maintain that *A* took longer than *B!*

He may say that *A* took longer because it is ahead of *B* or that *B* took a shorter time because it didn't have so far to go. In either case, he is centering on the spatial characteristics of the event and more particularly on spatial *states* (as opposed to transformations); whereas movement (distance), velocity, and time in an adult are all differen-tiated parts of a single cognitive structure. This structure begins to form in the Preoperational Subperiod, but it is thoroughly dominated by spatial perceptions.

[51] A more detailed account of the experiments on time, measurement, and velocity is available in Chapter 9 of Flavell's *The Developmental Psychology of Jean Piaget*, 1963. See especially pp. 316–326.

Thus in order to develop a conception of time, it is necessary to develop conceptions of movement and velocity. But in order to develop a conception of velocity, for example, it is necessary to develop a conception of time. It looks like a vicious circle; but before we give up, let's take a closer look at the child's conception of velocity.

Velocity is a relation between time and movement. We have seen how the young child deals with time; now let's test his conception of movement—i.e., the spatial displacement of an object in his visual field.

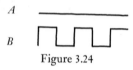

Figure 3.24

The child is told that the two lines in Figure 3.24 are streetcar tracks, and that any small object moved along it is a streetcar. The experimenter moves a "car" over a given number of segments of Track *B* and asks the child to make a trip of the same length on *A* with his car.

The child probably will move his car to a position opposite that of the experimenter, which of course means that his trip has actually been less than half as long. The early Preoperational child will continue to respond in this way even when supplied with a piece of cardboard exactly equal in length to a segment of Track *B*.

This performance seems to have one characteristic in common with that of the time problem presented earlier. In both, there apparently is a centering on terminal spatial order—i.e., given simultaneous starts from identical points on the spatial dimension "left-to-right," the child's answer depends on which car is farther to the right at the end of the episode.

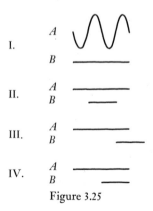

Figure 3.25

We suspect, then, that centering on terminal position is at least a part of the problem—a hypothesis that can be applied to velocity problems.

In Figure 3.25, *A* represents the route of one object, *B* that of another; the Roman numerals indicate different problems, each of which takes but a few seconds. In each of the four problems, the two objects start simultaneously and stop simultaneously. It is therefore obvious to an adult that in each problem, the velocity of Object *A* is greater than that of Object *B*.

But here are the responses of a subject in the Preoperational Subperiod:

In problem I the child says that "*A* and *B* travel at the same speed," which they don't.

In problem II, he says that "*A* is faster than *B*," which, of course, is correct.

In problem III, he says that "*B* is faster than *A*," which it is not.

In problem IV, he believes that "*A* is faster," which, like his response to problem II, is correct.

Thus II and IV are correct; I and III are not, since *A* is in fact faster than *B* in all four problems.

However, the interesting question in each case is, "Why?" All but one of these performances confirms the "terminal position" hypothesis. In I, II, and III, terminal position and perceived speed agree precisely, whereas in IV the hypothesis calls for a "same speed" response, and that is not what happens.

A slight variation in the experimental procedure gives us a clue to the reason for that exception. In this version of problem IV, the objects move through tunnels from their initial to their final positions. When this is done, the child does say that they move at the same speed; and that, of course, is in line with the "terminal position" hypothesis.

But why should the addition of the tunnel have this effect? Apparently there is another structure, "the passing schema," that dominates over terminal position when the two are in conflict. The "passing schema" is activated whenever one object is seen to overtake another (even if the action stops before an actual passing occurs). What the tunnel does is to prevent this structure from operating, so that the child then falls back onto his terminal position schema.

Thus, although centering on terminal position is not what deter-mines the response in all of the examples we have discussed here, there does seem to be a kind of centering that limits the competence of the Preoperational child in each one; and with the single exception of the "passing schema," that centering is on an end state rather than a transformation.

Shifting back to time for a moment, we find centering again when we ask a young child how old someone is compared to someone else. His reply will depend entirely upon the heights of the two persons judged. It might be regarded as a sort of "vertical terminal position" effect!

On page 88, we encountered a vicious circle in which the develop-ment of each of three concepts,

time	$(t = d/v)$,
movement	$(d = vt)$,
velocity	$(v = d/t)$,

is dependent on the development of each of the others. Have we broken out of that circle? I'm not sure that we have. As a matter of fact, the physicists themselves have had trouble with this one, though Piaget suggests that a breakthrough may be in the making. A French physicist has proposed that velocity be defined in terms of the notion of passing, which is precisely the way in which the Preoperation child "defines" it![52]

Summary

Since birth, the dominant mental activities of the child have changed from overt actions (in the Sensorimotor Period) to percep-tions (in the Preoperational Subperiod) to intellectual operations (in the Concrete Operations Subperiod). Those operations occur within a framework of class relations that make possible what Piaget calls *mobility* of thinking—reversibility, decentering, taking the view of the other, etc. As a result, the Concrete Operations child conserves quan-tity and number, constructs the time and space that he will live with as an adult, and establishes the foundations of the logical thinking that is the identifying feature of the next and final period of his development.

---

[52] Piaget, "The Child and Modern Physics," *Scientific American*, vol. 196, no. 3 (March 1957), p. 51.

IV

Formal Operations Period
(11-15 years)

IV

Formal Operations Period

Marvelous though they are when compared, for example, to the most advanced thinking of any subhuman species, Concrete Operations still fall far short of the intellectual accomplishments of an intelligent human adult. My purpose in this chapter is not to analyze these adult accomplishments in great detail, but rather to identify the crucial characteristics that differentiate them from earlier ones. Consequently, the chapter is relatively brief.

Another reason for the relative brevity of this chapter is that the characteristics of adult thinking are somewhat more accessible than are the processes discussed earlier. Every college course is an enterprise that requires a great deal of thinking; one who is looking for the *operations* involved in that thinking may be able to find some of them. A better way to focus attention on those operations would be to take a course in logic. Those who can arrange to include such a course in their curriculum should do so, but should look at it from a psychological viewpoint, remembering always the Piagetian dictum that *logic* is the mirror of *thought,* rather than vice versa. That is, the function of logic is to make explicit those mental processes that occur naturally at the highest level of human development.

Before turning the reader over to a logician, however, there are a few general things that I wish to say about the transition from Concrete to Formal Operations. I shall describe but a single problem, so that its implications may be examined in reasonable detail.

Archimedes' Law of Floating Bodies

An object will float if its specific gravity is less than 1.00—i.e., if its density is less than that of water. In an experimental test, this can be reduced to a comparison of the *weights of equal volumes* of the two substances. Some objects are able to derive this law while being questioned by the investigator. But by no means are all of them competent to do so, and the differences among them are correlated with differences in age.

Apparatus

The subject is presented with
    1) a bucket of water and
    2) several different objects, each small enough to fit into the
         bucket.[1]

Procedure

The subject is asked to classify the objects according to whether they will float and to explain the basis of his classification in each case. Then he is allowed to experiment with the materials and is asked to summarize his observations and to look for a *law* that will tie them all together.

Concrete Operations Applied to
the Floating Bodies Problem

My purpose in this section and in the following two sections ("Operations on Operations" and "The Real versus the Possible") is

---

[1] Subjects were also supplied with three cubes of different densities and an empty plastic cube to facilitate accurate comparisons with the density of water.

to analyze the behavior of school-age children and adolescents in the situation described above. I shall first present some examples of performances by subjects who are not yet in the Formal Operations Period.

Although the Preoperational child in this situation blithely invokes a special cause for each event, the Concrete Operations child is troubled by inconsistencies that had not troubled him earlier because they had not existed for him; he had lacked "instruments of coordination (operational classifications, etc.), which will attain equilibrium only at the point when concrete operations are structured."[2]

That equilibrium is not attained suddenly, but progress is made precisely because of the child's awareness that he is in difficulty. In the early part of the Concrete Operations Period, the main contradiction is that certain large objects will float and certain small ones sink. It is a contradiction because he begins the period with a kind of "absolute weight" concept as his main tool for dealing with the problem. Each object, including each bucket of water, has a "weight" that is conceived as a force that somehow opposes other forces, but in no consistent manner. (One moment he may predict that water will push a solid object up; the next moment, that it will push one down.) Initially, this "weight" is a quality of each separate object, not of the substance of which the object is constituted; hence the term "absolute weight."

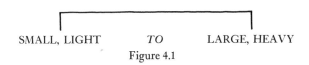

SMALL, LIGHT   *TO*   LARGE, HEAVY
Figure 4.1

Moreover, the child assigns a weight to an object by placing it on a scale something like that shown in Figure 4.1; size and weight are not discriminated as separate dimensions. That soon changes, however.

BAR [seven years, eleven months] first classifies the bodies into three categories: those that float because they are light [wood, matches, paper, and the aluminum cover]; those that sink because they are heavy [large

---

[2]Barbel Inhelder and Jean Piaget, *The Growth of Logical Thinking from Childhood to Adolescence,* translated by Anne Parson and S. Milgram, New York, Basic Books, Inc., 1958, p. 28. (Original French edition, 1955.)

and small keys, pebbles of all sizes, ring clamps, needles and nails, a metal cylinder, and an eraser]; and those that remain suspended at a midway point [fish].

"The needle?"

"It goes down because it's iron."

"And the key?"

"It sinks too."

"And the small things?" [nails, ring clamps].

"They are iron too."

"And this little pebble?"

"It's heavy because it's stone."

"And the little nail?"

"It's just a little heavy."

"And the cover, why does it stay up?"

"It has edges and sinks if it's filled with water."

"Why?"

"Because it's iron."[3]

One process that seems to be going on here is the assimilation of new objects into established categories. The needle "goes down because it's iron"; the nails, ring clamps, and probably the key "are iron too." The pebble is "heavy because it's stone." Even the aluminum pan lid, which does not sink unless it is filled with water, is said to sink "because it's iron."

Although it does not always show in the protocols, children early in the Concrete Operations Subperiod often make a three-way "sinkability" classification. Some objects can be relied upon to float, others will surely sink, and still others may either float or sink, depending on the circumstances (e.g., the aluminum pan lid mentioned above).

The foregoing example (BAR, age seven years, eleven months) demonstrates the Concrete Operations child's ability to classify objects; but it also reveals a notable lack of refinement of the relevant structures. What the child needs as a foundation for the impending "opera-

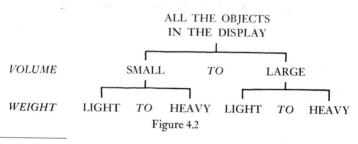

Figure 4.2

[3] *Ibid.*, p. 29.

tions on operations" stage is a structure something like that shown in Figure 4.2. Does he have it? Here is BAR again, thirteen months later:

BAR (nine years). [Class 1] Floating objects; ball, pieces of wood, corks, and an aluminum plate. [Class 2] Sinking objects: keys, metal weights, needles, stones, large block of wood, and a piece of wax. [Class 3] Objects that may either float or sink: covers. [Seeing] a needle at the bottom of the water [BAR] says:

"Ah! They are too heavy for the water, so the water can't carry them."

"And the tokens?"

"I don't know; they are more likely to go under."

"Why do these things float?" [Class 1]

"Because they are quite light."

"And the covers?"

"They can go to the bottom because the water can come up over the top."

"And why do these things sink?" [Class 2]

"Because they are heavy."

"The big block of wood?"

"It will go under."

"Why?"

"There is too much water for it to stay up."

"And the needles?"

"They are lighter."

"So?"

"If the wood were the same size as the needle, it would be lighter."

"Put the candle in the water. Why does it stay up?"

"I don't know."

"And the cover?"

"It's iron; that's not too heavy, and there is enough water to carry it."

"And now?" [It sinks.]

"That's because the water got inside."

"And put the wooden block in."

"Ah! Because it's wood that is wide enough not to sink."

"If it were a cube?"

"I think that it would go under."

"And if you push it under?"

"I think it would come back up."

"And if you push this plate?" [aluminum]

"It would stay at the bottom."

"Why?"

"Because the water weights on the plate."

"Which is heavier, the plate or the wood?"

"The piece of wood."

"Then why does the plate stay at the bottom?"

"Because it's a little lighter than the wood; when there is water on top there is less resistance and it can stay down. The wood has resistance, and it comes back up."

"And this little piece of wood?"

"No, it will come back up because it is even lighter than the plate."

"And if we begin again with this large piece of wood in the smallest bucket, will the same thing happen?"

"No, it will come back up because the water isn't strong enough: there is not enough weight from the water."[4]

I'm sure we can agree that BAR is pretty badly confused. He did, at one point near the beginning of the episode, hit upon an idea that might have been expanded into a solution: he said, "If the wood were the same size as the needle, it would be lighter." Why did he fail to develop this point? He failed because he still lacks the structure delineated in Figure 4.2. Instead of utilizing a general operational form in dealing with the relation of weight to volume, he is virtually limited to a particular case—the comparison of iron with wood. Moreover, when he does make comparisons, they are (with the single exception noted above) not comparisons of the weights of *equal volumes* of substances. The concept of specific gravity demands just such a comparison. But when BAR compares the weight of an object with that of water, he compares it with the entire quantity of water in the bucket; the same piece of wood will sink in one bucket, float in another.

Thus BAR, bothered by vaguely perceived inadequacies in his explanations, blunders energetically into one contradiction after another, until by the end of the session he has reverted to explanation by absolute weight.

It is a temporary regression, however. In general, the Concrete Operations child is much more orderly in his thinking than that. Even in the earlier session (seven years, eleven months) BAR classified the objects into three "sinkability" categories. And the third of those categories (objects that float or sink, depending on the circumstances) becomes further refined during the course of the subperiod:

RAY [nine years]: "The wood isn't the same as iron. It's lighter; there are holes in between." "And steel?" "It stays under because there aren't any holes in between."

DUM [nine years, six months]: The wood floats "because there is air inside"; the key does not "because there isn't any air inside."[5]

---

[4] *Ibid.*, p. 33.

[5] *Ibid.*, p. 35.

"Float-or-sink-depending-on-the-circumstances" has become "more-or-less-filled," and that serves the child quite well in his quest for reduction of inconsistencies.

On the other hand, since "the water" is for him the volume of all the water in the container rather than just that displaced by the object, the ultimate explicit comparison between a measured volume of water and an equal volume of the other substance does not occur. The Concrete Operations child has not yet elaborated the structure of Figure 4.2, in which weight and volume are dealt with as separate, interacting dimensions. That elaboration awaits the development of "formal operations," beginning at about eleven or twelve years of age.

Operations on Operations

When weight and volume do at last become operational, the adolescent can place them into a logical relationship to each other—a relation known as *proportion*:[6]

$$\frac{W_0}{V_0} = d,$$

where

W_0 is the weight of the object,
V_0 is the volume of the object, and
d is the density of the object.

If we assume that the object is "solid,"[7] it will float if

$$\frac{W_0}{V_0} < \frac{W_w}{V_w};$$

i.e., if its "specific gravity" is less than 1.00.

The important thing to note about all this is that the adolescent is

---

[6] Actually, volume conservation itself involves a proportion, since as one dimension of a solid is doubled, the product of the other two must be halved. If we start with a 2-inch cube, for example, the transformation will be:

$A_1 \times B_1 \times C_1 = A_1 (B_1 \times C_1) = 2 (2 \times 2) = 8$ cubic inches,
or
$A_2 \times B_2 \times C_2 = A_2 (B_2 \times C_2) = 4 (1 \times 2) = 8$ cubic inches.

[7] If the object is a vessel, then W must include weight of air contained below water line, and V must include volume of air contained below water line.

operating on operations. Piaget refers to *second-order operations,* and if my reading of him is correct, those operations constitute one of the fundamental characteristics of the Formal Operations Period. In the Piaget experiments, the concept of weight involves at least the operations of placing the object in a *series* from small to large gravity forces and of establishing a *correspondence* between that series and a series of inputs from the balance scale used to measure it. And the concept of volume requires similar operations—i.e., establishing correspondence between visual space and displacement of liquid. These are operations with objects, and they are necessary to the solution of the floating bodies problem. They are *necessary,* but not *sufficient.* The adolescent starts with these concrete operations, but then, in the floating bodies problem, he places them into a logical relationship to each other (a proportion); that is, he *operates on the operations.*

The Real Versus The Possible

As he grows older and gains more experience, the child's construction of reality becomes more precise and extended, and that makes him aware of gaps in his understanding that had been masked by the vagueness of his previous constructions. He fills those gaps with *hypotheses,* and he is able to formulate—and often even to test —hypotheses without actually manipulating concrete objects.

The following examples illustrate formal operations in the floating bodies problem:

FRAN [twelve years, one month] does not manage to discover the law, but neither does he accept any of the earlier hypotheses. He classifies correctly the objects presented here but hesitates before the aluminum wire.

"Why are you hesitating?"

"Because of the lightness, but no, that has no effect."

"Why?"

"The lightness has no effect. It depends on the sort of matter: for example, the wood can be heavy, and it floats." And for the cover: "I thought of the surface."

"The surface plays a role?"

"Maybe, the surface that touches the water, but that doesn't mean anything."

Thus he discards all of his hypotheses without finding a solution.

FIS [twelve years, six months] also . . . comes close to solution, saying in reference to a penny that it sinks "because it is small, it isn't stretched enough . . . . You would have to have something larger to stay at the surface, something of the same weight and which would have a greater extension."[8]

Observe the difference between these performances and those of the Concrete Operations child. There is a kind of transcendence of the immediate here—a systematic trying out of possibilities. These subjects actually formulate hypotheses about the problem.

A child in the Concrete Operations Subperiod does not formulate hypotheses. His accommodations are to events in the real world; he can only classify[9] objects or events, place them in serial relationship to each other, and establish a correspondence of units in different categories. Tall children are older than shorter ones; tall dolls get tall sticks; greater movement of a spring balance means heavier weight; and so on. It is true that the ability to do these things implies a cognitive framework into which yet-to-be-experienced events can be placed,[10] but the possible is always a limited an direct extension of concrete realty—a kind of generalization of existing structures to new content.

At the age of twelve, however, we find FRAN trying out *hypotheses* in his mind and discarding them as inappropriate, without any necessity of actually manipulating materials. FIS transforms the "more-or-less-filled" category of the Concrete Operations Period into a relationship between the weight-to-volume ratio of the object and the weight-to-volume ratio of water. And at age fourteen, another subject (WYR) actually manipulates one variable systematically while holding all others constant, which of course is the classical method of experimental science.

The Preoperational child is capable of preposterous flights of fancy; the Concrete Operations child's thinking is limited by his concern for organizing the actual data of his senses. The adolescent in the Period of Formal Operations is like both of these and different from each; he is capable of departures from reality, but those departures are lawful; he is concerned with reality, but reality is only a subset within a much larger set of possibilities.

---

[8] *The Growth of Logical Thinking from Childhood to Adolescence*, 1958, pp. 37–38.

[9] Classifying includes counting.

[10] For example, if he built a structure in which $A < B < C$, he can extend the series to D, E, F, etc. Or if $A < C < E$, he may interpolate B and D.

Egocentrism

The introduction to "possibilities" has a curious side effect. The subject's thinking becomes *egocentric*. The term "egocentrism" is usually used by Piaget scholars to refer to one outstanding characteristic of a child's thinking while he is in the Preoperational Subperiod of the Concrete Relations Period. In truth, however, Piaget says that there are not one, but three times in a person's life when his thinking takes on this character.

The three major periods of development—Sensorimotor, Concrete Operations, and Formal Operations—represent three different fields of cognitive action, and at the beginning of each, there is a relative lack of structural differentiation and functional equilibrium. To the neonate, the world is his *actions* upon it; to the Preoperational child, his *representations* of the world of physical objects are the only ones possible. The adolescent's egocentrism results from the extension of his thinking into the realm of the *possible* through the instruments of propositional logic. He fails "to distinguish between the ego's new and unpredicted capacities and the social or cosmic universe to which they are applied."[11] He goes through a phase during which his own cerebration seems to him omnipotent, and it is this at time that he is likely to annoy his elders with all sorts of idealistic schemes designed to bring reality into line with his own thinking.

"Formal" as Pertaining to "Form"

You should now be in a position to appreciate the significance of the title "Formal Operations." It refers to the fact that the adolescent can follow the form of an argument but disregard its specific content. Younger children are not able to do that. If, for example, we present to a Concrete Operations child the following sentence:

"I am very glad I do not [like] onions, for

if I liked them, I would always be eating them, and

I hate eating unpleasant things,"

---

[11] *The Growth of Logical Thinking from Childhood to Adolescence*, 1958, p. 345.

he will respond to the *content* of the sentence by saying, in effect:

> "Onions are unpleasant; it is wrong not to like them"; and so on.

The adolescent, on the other hand, will respond to the *form* of the argument by focusing on the contradiction between

> "if I liked them" and

> "onions are unpleasant."[12]

Or take the syllogism

> "All children like spinach;
>
> boys are children;
>
> therefore boys like spinach."

The younger child will respond to the content (particularly if he is a boy who doesn't like spinach!), but the adolescent can follow the argument[13] because he is impressed by its form.

Summary

Let us now summarize what has been said about the Formal Operations Period. The adolescent begins where the Concrete Operations child left off—with *concrete operations*. He then *operates on those operations* by casting them into the form of propositions. These

---

[12] The example is a nonsense-sentence by Ballard, quoted in Hunt's *Intelligence and Experience*, 1961, p. 232. The first line of the Hunt quotation of Ballard actually reads, "I am very glad I do not *eat* onions,..." (italics mine). Since I was unable to locate the original, I hope both the reader and Dr. Hunt will forgive the substitution of "like" for "eat." I am reasonably certain that the latter is an error of transcription.

[13] He can, but that doesn't mean that he necessarily does. Morgan and Morton (*Journal of Social Psychology*, 1944) presented college students with the following syllogism: "Some ruthless men deserve a violent death. Since one of the most ruthless men was Heydrich, the Nazi hangman, therefore:
    1. Heydrich, the Nazi hangman, deserved a violent death.
    2. Heydrich may have deserved a violent death.
    3. Heydrich did not deserve a violent death.
    4. None of these conclusions logically follows.
Thirty-seven percent of the subjects chose number one!

propositions then become a part of a cognitive structure that owes its existence to past experience but makes possible hypotheses that do not correspond to any particular experience. The Concrete Operations child always starts with experience and makes limited interpolations and extrapolations from the data available to his senses. The adolescent, however, begins with the *possible* and then checks various possibilities against memorial representations of past experience, and eventually against sensory feedback from the concrete manipulations that are suggested by his hypotheses.

Finally, to say that cognition is relatively independent of concrete reality is to say that the *content* of a problem has at last been subordinated to the *form* of relations within it.

Now is the time for a review of Chapter I.
See explanation in Preface.

V

Educational Implications:
An Epilogue

V

Educational Implications:
An Epilogue

When Piaget began his study of genetic epistemology nearly fifty years ago, probably the farthest thing from his mind was its "educational implications." He was concerned with how cognitions develop, not with developing cognitions. His writings are not addressed to educators—or even to psychologists, for that matter. He is an interdisciplinary thinker, and his main concerns are still, much as they were in the beginning, theoretical rather than practical. Although he has occasionally commented on educational practices (as virtually everyone has, in his own way), to my knowledge he has never touted his theory as the basis of a new pedagogy.

All that is entirely fitting, as far as it goes. But after all, Piaget has said some pretty important things about children, and anyone who says important things about children ultimately must be important to educators. Teaching is the manipulation of the student's environment in such a way that his activities will contribute to his development (toward goals whose definitions are not our present concern). It should be obvious to the reader by now that the effect of a given environment on a child is as much a function of the child as of the environment. If a teacher knows that, his behavior will be affected by his conception of what students are like. Indeed, his very definition of teaching will be so determined. Mine was.

In this chapter, I shall present some principles and some practices. The practices have not necessarily emerged from the principles—certainly not from my statement of them, which appears here for the first time. Two of the "examples" (Sigel and Hooper; Pinard and Laurendeau) are virtually direct applications of Piaget's ideas; the other two (Kephart; Suchman) are the products of the general theoretical trend (Preface, p. *vii*) that has supported Piaget's work, but not of that work itself. Finally, the illustrations are in no way exhaustive of those that could be cited; nor is each necessarily the best that could have been chosen (though I certainly regard them as among the best available at this time). We shall consider the implications of the theory for two professions within the field of education; teaching and testing.

Teaching: Principles

Piaget has not constructed a theory of teaching: that much is clear. But the theory is about intellectual development, and since most teaching has a similar concern, there should be some overlap between the two. Is there? Granted that the theory does not say anything about interventions as such, does it say anything that is pertinent to the concerns of those who would intervene in child development?

I think it does. The following five principles have been derived from the theory and are stated here as laconically as possible; they are intended as reminders of some things that by this time the reader should know. No prescriptions for teacher behavior are given here, but to the extent that teacher behavior is influenced by a knowledge of what goes on in the minds of their students, these principles should prove helpful.

Action

The brain is not a passive receptacle, but an active, organizing, dynamic system. Every pattern of input must be run through the filter of existing structures, and at the same time every such encounter changes those structures. In a word, cognition is action.[1]

At first, the actions are almost entirely overt; later, they are internalized in the form of simple representations of concrete objects and events; and finally, they become organized into the complex networks that underlie logical thinking in the adult.

Sequence and Integration of Structures

Each new cognitive structure depends upon—indeed, is made up of—other structures that developed earlier. Understanding is not possible without a structural base, and that base must be constructed out of available materials.

With the exception of the reflexes present at birth, structures are never "given," no matter how obvious they may seem to an adult; and unless these "obvious" structures have been constructed through experience (in a sufficiently mature organism), no amount of training will produce the higher levels of understanding to which educational enterprises are committed. Once a basic structure has been learned, however, it will continue to function intermittently through subsequent periods of development.

Structure and Transfer

A cognitive structure is a more or less tightly organized system of mental actions. New inputs that are congruent with an existing structure are organized by it (assimilated to it). When a child finds himself in a new situation, he thinks about it in terms of the system of mental actions that he brings to that situation. Thus, although there may be some direct transfer of relatively unstructured associations, most effects of prior learning are effects of experience on cognitive structures.

A structure (understanding, principle) then serves to organize new knowledge; conversely, the new situation may modify the structure. Both are facilitated by extensive "application" of new knowledge.

---

[1] This probably ought to be called a "proposition" rather than a "principle." It is included because it is a proposition of fundamental importance both to the theory and to educational practice.

Optimal Discrepancy

If input is precisely congruent with established cognitive structure, new learning does not occur; and if the input does not fit into the structure at all, it is simply not assimilated. The optimal difficulty of a task is therefore one in which the complexity of the child's cognitive structure almost, but not quite, matches that of the input pattern. Given those conditions, the structure will change.

Motivation

It is the nature of the brain to be active. Even when cognitive structures are in relative equilibrium, the equilibrium is a dynamic one in which the structures (1) assimilate all the input they are capable of organizing and (2) accommodate to input patterns if they are already almost congruent. Therefore, if the discrepancy between the new input and the established structure is within the optimal range, learning will occur without external reinforcement.

Teaching: Examples

The events presented in this section are described in considerable detail. At the conclusion of each subsection, I have made a few brief comments about principles, but the reader should try to keep the principles in mind while reading the examples.

Preparing the Sensorimotor Child for Preoperational Thinking: Kephart's "Perceptual Remediation"[2]

Dr. Newell C. Kephart for many years directed a program of research at Purdue University that inquired into the relationship of sensorimotor constructions to intellectual performance. From this research, Dr. Kephart concluded, as had Piaget before him, that normal

---

[2] My term, not Kephart's.

sensorimotor development is a prerequisite to orderly symbolic functioning.

His studies indicate that the infant develops a kind of internal map, or "body image," that is based initially upon his discrimination of "laterality"—i.e., the distinction of right from left. The resulting internal map is then gradually extended to encompass the space that surrounds him and to include the quality of "directionality." ("Directionality" is the exterior counterpart of the internal "laterality.") Each of these "maps" is actually a program for the control of behavior—a closed system in which the output is continually fed back into the system. This self-monitoring system is sensorimotor, or, as Kephart puts it, "perceptual-motor."

The perception of form, for example, is largely a construction of relationships among visual elements, and the construction occurs within a spatial framework. The child who has failed to develop that spatial framework will inevitably have difficulty with form perception and with all those scholastic activities (notably reading) that depend upon form perception. Therefore, when a child does have such difficulty, Kephart and his colleagues suspect a weakness in form perception. And when that suspicion is confirmed, they prescribe remedial activities that are essentially sensorimotor; because space is primarily a sensorimotor construction.

Kephart and his co-workers have developed a number of techniques for dealing with sensorimotor deficiencies. One of them is known as "the walking board." The apparatus consists of a piece of two-by-four, eight to twelve feet in length, supported on either end by a substantial bracket that holds the board about two inches off the floor and prevents it from tipping. The bracket can be adjusted to hold the board with either the two-inch or the four-inch dimension uppermost as a walking surface for the child; the four-inch surface is used for beginners or for those children who have special difficuty with the narrower surface. The child's first task is merely to walk slowly from one end of the board to the other.

The walking board had been used in kindergartens and elementary schools long before Kephart took it up, but he warns his reader to

> ... remember, however, that the contribution of the walking board results from its implications for teaching balance and laterality rather than in the development of skill on the walking board itself . . . .[3]

---

[3] N. C. Kephart, *The Slow Learner in the Classroom*, Columbus, Ohio: Charles E. Merrill Publishing Co., 1960, p. 218.

If the task is too difficult, it is made easier by turning the board on its side, holding the child's hand, or even substituting a larger board; but it must not be made too easy either:

> ...The child who walks across the board and does not lose his balance is not learning from the activity. Only when he loses his balance and is required to correct it, does he learn.... We must [therefore] see that he does not avoid the problem by running or otherwise changing the procedure.[4]

Once he has mastered the forward walk, he is asked to do the same thing backward. He may need adult help at first, but he is encouraged to dispense with it as quickly as possible. Also

> ...He is allowed to look back to see where the next step should be but is encouraged to learn where the board is behind him without having to look.... He may have to explore with his toe before each step to locate the board behind him. He is allowed to do this but is encouraged to learn the direction "straight back" so that such preliminary explorations will no longer be necessary.[5]

Walking backward is followed by walking sideways, and then by starting forward in one direction and turning round at the middle; and finally:

> The most difficult task is to walk backward across the board, turn, and return walking backward. This...requires maintaining the difficult backward directionality while turning.[6]

Additional combinations of forward and backward walking may be devised, and bouncing (on the flexible middle portion of the board) may be added. All of these require that the child maintain his balance "under conditions that, for him, are unusual. Thus, he learns to maintain balance under conditions which cannot be completely foreseen."[7]

Other techniques have been described: standing on a large, flat board balanced on a three-by-three inch post; jumping on a trampoline;

---

[4] *Ibid.*, p. 218.

[5] *Ibid.*, pp. 218–219.

[6] *Ibid.*, p. 219.

[7] *Ibid.*, p. 219.

doing a kind of horizontal calisthenics in which the heels and wrists are in contact with the floor at all times (to magnify feedback from the movements); and many others.[8] The simplest of these are designed to emphasize laterality; the most complex require the maintenance of laterality and directionality through abnormal alterations of "postural and balance relationships."[9]

Normally, a child's "natural" environment provides the necessary stimulation for these constructions to occur within approximately the first two years of his life. When interventions are conceived by Kephart and his co-workers, they are usually remedial—i.e., they are imposed because some deficiency has been observed in a child considerably older than two years. Such deficiencies do occur, and if the requisite foundations have not been solidly built during the first two years, it may be necessary for the sake of future development to confront the older child with the necessity of accommodating his inadequate cognitive structure to the structure of the world about him.

Each of these demands may be considered a discrepant event. That is, every time the child begins to lose his balance, for example, unfamiliar kinesthetic inputs must be assimilated. They will be assimilated if the event is not too discrepant; and in the process, the established structure will be changed (accommodated). In order to keep discrepancies within the optimal range, a careful sequence must be observed; once a structure has accommodated to unfamiliar inputs, it is capable of assimilating events that would previously have been too discrepant to be assimilated. Every time this occurs, we are justified in speaking of positive transfer (though we may be more impressed by the transfer that occurs between developmental periods). Because the discrepancy between inputs and established structures is maintained at nearly optimal range, motivation remains high; and of course —even more obviously here than in other developmental periods—the child is constantly active.

Although Kephart is not known as a "Piaget scholar" and did in fact develop his system independently (as independently as is possible for one who is familiar with the work of others in his field), the two theories—Piaget's and Kephart's—are similar enough in relevant particulars that the techniques described above might have been derived from either one.

---

[8] *Ibid.*, pp. 222–239.

[9] *Ibid.*, p. 234.

Preparing the Preoperational Child
for Concrete Operations:
A Controlled Experiment

One of the most notable achievements of the Concrete Operations Period—one that Piaget has characterized as "a necessary condition for all rational activity"[10]—is that of *conservation*. The conservation structure is developed and successfully applied to many different contents during that period. The example given here—a recent study by Sigel, Roeper, and Hooper[11]—will be evaluated in terms of a specified few of those—"substance," "liquid substance," "weight," and "volume";[12] but what will be attempted during the training sessions will be nothing short of conservation in general—at least at the level of concrete operations—and it will be attempted with children of age five or younger.

Treatment and control groups, five children in each, are matched on IQ (means ranging from 144 to 152 in the treatment and control groups of both experiments), chronological age (means ranging from four years, three months, to nearly five years), social status, and educational level. All are given the traditional Piagetian tests for conservation, once immediately before the beginning and once two weeks after the end of the training series.

The grand objective of that series is conservation, but there are important subgoals that must be specified before the training begins—especially since at no time during the training will any direct practice be given on the specific tasks that are used in testing. Sigel, Roeper, and Hooper predict that conservation will occur spontaneously if the child can master the operations of which it is composed.[13] Those opera-

---

[10] Jean Piaget and Alina Szeminska, *The Child's Conception of Number*, translated by C. Gattegno and F. M. Hodgson, New York: Humanities Press, 1952, p. 3. (Original French edition, 1941.)

[11] Irving E. Sigel, Annemarie Roeper, and Frank H. Hooper, "A Training Procedure for acquisition of Piaget's Conservation of Quantity: A Pilot Study and its Replication," *British Journal of Educational Psychology*, vol. 36, 1966, pp. 301–311. (Reprinted in Irving E. Sigel and Frank H. Hooper, *Logical Thinking in Children: Research Based on Piaget's Theory*, New York: Holt, Rinehart and Winston, Inc., 1968.)

[12] They use the term "substance" for what we have called "quantity"; "quantity" for them is a generic category that includes all four of those mentioned above. "Volume" conservation is of course not expected until the Formal Operations Period.

[13] Piaget has some reservations about this relationship. See his *Six Psychological Studies* (edited by David Elkind), New York: Random House, Inc., 1967, p. 114.

tions are (1) multiple classifications, (2) multiple relationality, and (3) reversibility.

You will recall that the Preoperational child tends to be dominated by his perceptions, to center on a single attribute of a display, and to "reason" transductively. In order to conserve, he must shake off that domination and rise above those limitations. He must decenter, and he must realize that an object can change in one respect without changing in other respects. He must learn that the object may be classified successively into many different categories of a single attribute, that it may be classified simultaneously on more than one attribute, that it may be compared to another object on more than one dimension, and that every transformation is reversible.

Which of those acquisitions do you think is (are?) the teacher's objective(s) in this training session?

TEACHER: Can you tell me what this is, Mary?

MARY: A banana.

TEACHER: What else can you tell me about it?

MARY: It's straight.

TEACHER: It's straight. What else?

MARY: It has a peel.

TEACHER: It has a peel .... Tom, what can you tell me about it?

TOM: Ummm ... It has some dark lines on it.

TEACHER: Uh-huh.

TOM: It has some green on it.

TEACHER: What can you do with it?

TOM: You can eat it!

TEACHER: That's right! ... Now let's see ...

CHILDREN: ... I love bananas!

TEACHER: What is this?

CHILDREN: An orange.

TEACHER: Is it really an orange?

CHILDREN: Uh-huh. ... Yes.

TEACHER: Look at it closely.

CHILD: It's an artificial one.

TEACHER: Oh, that's right, it's an artificial one ... But what else can you tell me about it?

CHILDREN: You can eat it ... It is round ...

TEACHER: Uh-huh.

CHILDREN: ... Orange.

TEACHER: That's right!

CHILD: It has a stem.

TEACHER: Now, look at this one . . . What's this?

CHILDREN: An orange . . . orange.

TEACHER: And what can you do with it?

CHILDREN: You can eat it . . . and it's round . . .

TEACHER: It is round . . . .

CHILD: It has a peel . . . .

TEACHER: It has a peel . . . Now, look at these two things. Are they the same?

CHILDREN: No.

TEACHER: What's different?

CHILDREN: This one . . . this one here is pressed in on the side a little . . . this one is lighter.

TEACHER: Do you know what this really is? This is a tangerine . . . and this is an orange. Now tell me in what ways they are alike.

CHILDREN: This is smaller and that's bigger.

TEACHER: I said, "In what way are they alike?"

CHILDREN: They are both round . . . they both have a stem . . . both orange.

TEACHER: They both have a stem, both round, both orange: Anything else alike about them?

CHILD: They're both fat.

TEACHER: Uh-huh. What can you do with them?

CHILDREN: We can eat them . . . .

TEACHER: We can eat them . . . Now, tell us, what's the same about all these things?

CHILD: These are round, but this isn't.

TEACHER: I said, what is the same about them, not what's different about them.

CHILDREN: They're both round . . . they're round . . . they're round . . . and they are both artificial.

TEACHER: They're all artificial, and, . . . are they all round?

CHILD: No.

TEACHER: What about the banana?

CHILD: It's straight.

TEACHER: But, . . . tell me something else that's the same about all of these things.

CHILD: . . . They have . . . all a peel.

TEACHER: That's right, too, but what can you do with all of them?

CHILDREN: You can eat them!

TEACHER: That's right! That's the same about every one of them. Do you have a name for all of them?

CHILDREN: Yes!

TEACHER: What?

CHILD: A banana.

TEACHER: A banana? No, . . . is there something that you can call all of them?

CHILDREN: Fruit . . . fruit.

TEACHER: And what's the same about all fruit?

CHILDREN: They are all round except bananas.

TEACHER: No, . . . why do you call all of these things fruit?

CHILDREN: Because you can eat them.

TEACHER: You can eat them.

CHILDREN: And they are food.

TEACHER: And they are food. If I had a piece of bread here, would that be fruit too?

CHILDREN: No.

TEACHER: Why not?

CHILDREN: Because it is not sweet . . . not round . . .

TEACHER: Because it is not sweet. I think that's a good reason . . . and, you eat bread too?

CHILDREN: Yes.

TEACHER: But is still not a fruit . . . right?

CHILDREN: Yes.

TEACHER: Now, can you tell me again what this is? We talked about it yesterday.

CHILD: A pencil.

TEACHER: What else can you tell me about it?

CHILDREN: It's round. . . . You said you were going to put it in . . .

TEACHER: That's right . . . Ah . . . Tom, what is this?

TOM: Chalk.

TEACHER: What else can you tell me about it?

TOM: It's white.

TEACHER: Gail, tell me, what's the same about these two things?

GAIL: They're both round.

TEACHER: What else?

GAIL: . . . . . . Ummm . . .

TEACHER: John, tell me, what's the same about these two things?

JOHN: . . . both write.

TEACHER: That's right! There are two things that are the same about
them. Tell me what they are?

JOHN: Well.....I don't know...

TEACHER: What are they, Mary?

MARY: They're round and they write.

TEACHER: Very good![14]

This process of identifying attributes, labeling categories, and defining
the criteria of class membership continues until the possibilities have
been exhausted. The teacher draws the children's attention to the
similarities and the differences between objects, with a view toward
developing a mechanism that can deal systematically with their attributes, taken one at a time.

After that, the emphasis is shifted to the relationships among different categories. Classifications are requested that require the coordination of two criteria—e.g., "Can you think of two things that you are
at the same time?" Considering the egocentrism of the Preoperational
child, that is a good place to begin such questioning; later, the same
demands are made with respect to nonpersonal objects.[15] Note that in
neither this nor the previous instance does the teacher impose the
classification system on the children; they build their own. But the
teacher is more than a mirror; he directs the inquiry in more subtle
ways.[16]

Finally, reversibility is introduced by dispersing a set of objects
and then reforming the set. A stack of pennies is divided among the
children, and each displays his collection in front of him on the table
for all to see. Regardless of how it has been divided, the original set of
pennies is then reproduced by gathering together all of its subsets.

As in the Kephart example, the subjects are continually active.
Moreover, the design of the experiment is such that they are tested in

---

14 "A Training Procedure for Acquisition of Piaget's Conservation of Quantity,"
pp. 305–306.

15 *Ibid.*, p. 300.

16 The teacher himself may not always appear to be totally decentered. Research
on "functional fixedness" has shown that adults often fail to reclassify objects even
when it is in their interest to do so. In one example, the subject stands between
two strings that are attached to the ceiling; his task is to tie the two free-hanging
ends together. They are far enough apart so that if he grasps one in one hand, it
is impossible for him to reach the other. The solution is to attach a weight to one
of the strings and start it swinging; then he can simply stand and wait for it to
come to him. A subject demonstrates functional fixedness when he fails to use as
a weight some object—e.g., a pair of pliers—that is normally used for some other
purpose or function (hence "functional fixedness").

a different situation than any of them have faced during the training and that the behavioral manifestations of any structural change will be detectable in the superiority of the training group in the testing situation. That is, there will be transfer. The design also emphasizes interdependence of structures, since the structure responsible for the subjects' behavior during the test situation is dependent upon—indeed, is made up of—those developed during training. The teacher's questions certainly are discrepant events for the child, because they demand that he look at familiar objects in unfamiliar ways. Motivation should be high if the discrepancy is near optimal; and apparently it is, for the tape recordings make it obvious that the children are highly motivated.

The Sigel, Roeper, and Hooper project differs from the other two examples in this section in at least two related ways: (1) it is carefully designed to test the implications of a theory rather than to improve the human condition and (2) it is a specific study (and its replication) rather than a prototype representing an unknown number of actual events; it is unique. For those reasons, it is feasible to report its results even though I shall make no attempt to do so for the Kephart and Suchman examples.

If we discount, then, the child Martha in the Training Group, and Em in the Control Group, who had shown pretest conservation, we find that the children in the first Training Group who had no conservation did acquire conservation ability, whereas this was not the case in the Control Group. The children who show no such ability are able to solve conservation problems only after the training experiences. This suggests that the testing situation may not be an influence unless some ability to profit from the experience is present. Combining the two samples [the original study and its replication], eight training and seven control subjects indicated pretest nonconservation. There were no post-test successes for any of the seven control subjects. In contrast, of the eight training subjects, five conserved substance, three conserved liquid substance, five conserved weight, and one subject succeeded on the volume task. Pass-fail contingency comparisons show differences between training and control performances on the substance and weight, e.g., Fisher Probability Test significance level of .025.[17]

And, in addition to the quantitative pass-fail comparisons, the trained subjects were judged to be better able "to verbalize the underlying

---

[17] "A Training Procedure for Acquisition of Piaget's Conservation of Quantity," p. 309.

operations and the salient dimensions of the criterion test situation."[18]

Thus it is clear that the training was effective. What did the trained subjects learn? They were trained specifically to classify objects successively into different categories of a single attribute, to classify them simultaneously on several attributes, and to recognize the reversibility of transformations within a set of objects. But as the foregoing example shows, the tests by which the training is evaluated are not tests of those specific functions; they are tests of conservation of quantity.

Conservation of quantity is one of the identifying characteristics and one of the most significant achievements of the Concrete Operations Subperiod. If the same results can be obtained in the training of other concrete operations, it may be possible to accelerate a young child's progress toward that level of mental development.

Preparing the Concrete Operations Child for Formal Operations and Giving Practice in Formal Operations: Suchman's "Inquiry Training"

In one of his rare pronouncements on education, Piaget recently quoted with approval a friend who had said, "Every time you teach a child something you keep him from reinventing it."[19] That could have been the takeoff point for the technique that I am about to describe.

It wasn't. Several years before Piaget quoted his friend's remark,[20] J. Richard Suchman had launched The Illinois Studies in Inquiry Training. The basic premise of the Illinois Training is that if the environment is responsive to his actions, a child will "invent" the cognitive structures necessary to integrate the information that is thereby made available.

The teacher is a part of a student's environment, however; and he is potentially a very important part, because he has knowledge of many pertinent events that are unknown to the student and cannot be arranged conveniently for his immediate observation. The problem is

---

[18] *Ibid.*, p. 305.

[19] Unpublished lecture at New York University, March 21, 1967.

[20] To the best of my knowledge, that is. He has used that quotation in at least two lectures in the United States, one delivered in Berkeley and one in New York. There may have been others.

to make use of the teacher's expertise without interfering with the student's creative activity.

Suchman's solution is to use the teacher primarily as a source of facts rather than of structures relating to those facts. Since the teacher almost certainly is predisposed to deal with the latter, he is expressly forbidden to do so during an inquiry session; he may respond only to questions framed in such a way that each may be answered with a simple "Yes" or "No."

An inquiry session may begin with a short film designed as a "discrepant event"; that is, the structure of the event depicted in the film is discrepant with the cognitive structure that the student has available for its interpretation. Assimilation of the input requires accommodation of the cognitive structure.

The accommodation is, as Piaget would have insisted it must be, a result of the student's activity. In this case, the child asks questions designed to explore further the set of conditions that gave rise to a discrepant event and to test hypotheses about the way in which the event is related to the conditions. Here is an example:

> One of the films is about a bimetal blade. When it is heated it bends downward, and when it is inserted into a tank of water, it straightens out. The demonstrator turns it over and puts it back on the flame. This time it bends upward, and when placed in water it once more straightens out. To the children who do not know anything about a bimetal blade, this is a discrepant event. They continue from there, using "yes" or "no" questions. They cannot ask, "Was it because?" If they start such questioning we tell them that it is their job to find explanations. "See if you can construct a theory. If you have one, you ought to be able to test it experimentally." Their experiments, too, are conducted through "yes" and "no" questions. "If we put the blade into a refrigerator would the same thing happen?" Such a question is the equivalent of an empirical test of a hypothesized relationship. The responsive environment is created by the teacher who answers the questions. As the children ask questions they build little theories that they test themselves.[21]

The student is always active, and motivation is intrinsic because the episode begins with an event that is discrepant with established structure. The teacher's choice of an initiating event must take into account

[21] J. Richard Suchman, "The Illinois Studies in Inquiry Training," *Journal of Research in Science Teaching*, vol. 2, 1964, pp. 231–232.

lawful sequences in development and the interdependence of structures, for in the absence of such considerations, he might choose an event that strays too far from optimal discrepancy. The student views the film; attempts to cognize the event portrayed in it; analyzes the event in order to specify discrepancies; forms hypotheses that would, if true, resolve the discrepancies; and finally, tests those hypotheses by asking questions of fact that are derived from them. The resulting structures may be expected to operate in somewhat different situations without specific training.

It occurs to me that Piaget's friend might better have used "tell" than "teach," in the remark cited at the beginning of this section.[22] There is a great deal more to teaching than just telling students what they ought to know.

Testing

Piaget's theory is based upon extensive observations of the behavior of children and adolescents. His method of observation is quite different from that of traditional mental testing; but both are systematic, and both are concerned with mental development. It should therefore not be at all surprising to find that a new test is currently being standardized—a test that has its roots in Piaget's theory and incorporates his method.

The new test ("scale of mental development") is the product of a program of research initiated several years ago by Adrien Pinard and his colleagues in the laboratory of genetic psychology at the University of Montreal.[23] The product is an attempt to combine the advantages of Piaget's method (thoroughness and flexibility of questioning) with those of traditional psychometric methods (standardization of questioning).

---

[22]Piaget delivered the lecture in French; it is possible that some distortion occurred in the process of translation into English. My source was a typescript in English, courtesy of a personal communication by Dr. Frank G. Jennings, who cautioned me that the translation was by no means "official," as it had not been approved by Piaget.

[23]Adrien Pinard and Monique Laurendeau "A Scale of Mental Development Based on the Theory of Piaget," *Journal of Research in Science Teaching*, vol. 2, 1964, pp. 253–260.

A New Kind of Intelligence Test

Most intelligence tests today do not make any direct use of the concept of "mental age."[24] Actually, however, they are all descendants of the original Binet scale, in which mental age was the very heart of the whole process. But the concept of mental age bears little relationship to the Piagetian "stage" of development, so a Piagetian test would necessarily be different in a very important way. If we were to compare the new test with the Stanford-Binet, for example, we would find that in the latter, items have met a statistical criterion of discrimination between chronological age groups; that is, older subjects have tended to pass them, younger ones to fail them. The difficulty level of any item is the chronological age of the youngest group of subjects who can pass it.

In contrast, the first step in the Montreal test has been a thorough study of intellectual development—a study based upon and including Piaget's own observations. Test items have been derived from that study and from the theory that spawned it. They have been designed specifically to reveal the dominant aspects of each stage of development. Only after all that has been accomplished is a statistical analysis performed to ascertain the chronological age at which each ability is acquired.

The administration of a traditional intelligence test is highly structured. With few exceptions, the same questions are asked of every subject on each item of the test. (*A sample item:* Tell me what's wrong with the following sentence: "The judge said to the prisoner, 'You are to be hanged, and I hope it will be a warning to you!'") An exception would occur if an additional question were introduced when the response to the standard question has been ambiguous; for the purpose of every question is to classify the subject's response as "pass" or "fail." Once that has been done, the examiner moves on to the next item. Given the rationale of the previous paragraph, all that is as it should be.

But there is another rationale. If performance is conceived as a

---

[24] "Mental age" is a scale unit that was until recently the basis of scoring Stanford-Binet intelligence tests. The average child of four has a mental age of four; the average child of six has a mental age of six, etc. A child's IQ is the ratio of his mental age to his chronological age at the time of the test (MA/CA); e.g., if his test performance is equal to that of the average six-year-old but he is only five, his IQ will be 120. That is, 6/5 1.20 (the decimal is dropped). Although the "ratio IQ" is no longer used, the concept of mental age is still fundamental to all Binet-type testing.

manifestation of a stage in the evolution of intelligence instead of a statistical average, it becomes important to find out why a particular subject is responding in a particular way, even if that response is wrong; in fact, a wrong answer can be more revealing in the long term than a correct one. Each question presents an opportunity for the subject to respond in a manner that will reveal the quality of his thinking, and the content of each is determined by the subject's response to the preceding ones. (An "item" in the Montreal test is likely to consist of doing an "experiment" in view of the subject—e.g., the floating bodies problem—and then questioning him about what he has just seen.) The entire testing session is therefore much less rigidly structured than is customary in psychometrics.

"Psychometrics" means "psychological measurement," and measurement implies quantification. Quantification was alluded to above when we discussed the difficulty level of a conventional test item. It would be possible to make difficulty level count directly in the total score, but in the Stanford-Binet that is not done; instead, each item that is passed is given the same score, regardless of its difficulty. It is true that the items are arranged in order of increasing difficulty and that for any given subject records are kept only of those between the all-passed level and the all-failed level. But it is also true that within those limits it is possible to compensate for failing certain low-level items by passing certain high-level items.

The possibility of such compensations emphasizes the fact that a "mental age" from the Stanford-Binet is not a true genetic stage that depends for its existence upon a mastery of the acquisitions characteristic of all preceding stages. The final score is instead merely a sum of items passed in a series of generally increasing difficulty.

The scoring of the Montreal scale can be characterized quickly by contrasting it with that of the Stanford-Binet. Whereas the latter allows for compensatory achievements at higher levels than those at which failures already have occurred, the Montreal method usually requires classifying the subject into a developmental stage by means of a qualitative analysis of his performance. Whereas the final result of a Stanford-Binet test is a score determined by the number of items passed within a limited range of difficulty,[25] the issue of a Montreal test is a statement about the subject's level of intellectual development—a

---

[25] An experienced examiner may glean a great deal more information from the testing session, but it is not a part of the basic validation of the instrument.

Table III. Relation of Montreal Intelligence Test to Traditional Type

Characteristic of Test	Type of Test	
	Traditional	Montreal
Standardization	"Level" determined statistically.	"Level" derived from theory.
	Items selected that discriminate between specified chronological age groups.	Intellectual development studied; problems devised to reveal various levels of mental process. Statistical analysis, to determine average age of each acquisition, is done later.
Administration	Highly structured. With few exceptions, same questions asked of all subjects who respond to a given item.	Less structured. Each question determined by subject's answer to preceding ones.
	Exceptions are questions designed to clarify pass-fail distinction.	Questions designed to reveal quality of subject's thinking.
	Only right answers are important.	Wrong answers are important.
Scoring	Determined by number of items passed within a limited range of difficulty.	Determined by quality of responses to a standard set of items. "Level" is quality of response rather than difficulty of items passed.
	Failing an item at one level can be compensated for by passing one at a different level.	Items not passed or failed, but evaluated for stage inclusion.

statement that expresses the quality of his responses to a relatively small number of problem situations. Whereas the Stanford-Binet presents the same questions (within the appropriate range of difficulty) to all subjects, the Montreal test presents different, alternative questions to each subject. The choice in each case depends on the subject's responses to earlier questions.

The relationships discussed above are summarized in Table III on page 125.

Testing in the School

The prime objective of the Montreal research was to extend Piaget's observations to populations other than that of Geneva under conditions imposed by the canons of experimental method. Pinard and his colleagues wanted to know whether Piaget's stages would survive that kind of scrutiny. (In general, they did.) The development of an intelligence scale for use in the schools was only a by-product of a program of research in "pure" or "basic" science.

The fact remains that one result of that research has been an ordinal scale[26] of mental development applicable to children from two to twelve years of age. Like the "spin-off" of the NASA space program, the result could be as important a technological advance as if it had been sought directly.

We have already alluded to the potential effect of Piaget's theory on teaching. Nothing more need be said here, beyond simply pointing out that for the teacher who wishes to implement Piagetian ideas, it is essential to ascertain the developmental level of the students being taught. There are other ways in which that might be accomplished; teachers familiar with the theory can to some extent make their own judgments. But a standardized test could prove extremely helpful, especially if the teacher were able to converse in Piagetian terms with the specialist who administers the test.

It is clear that such a test would require the services of a specialist. Furthermore, a specialist would have to be more than a mere technician, for the unstructured format demands a thorough grounding in the theory that underlies each question. Who might the specialist be?

The person who is at once available and psychologically trained is the school psychologist. For the most part, training in school psychology has not included much acquaintance with Piaget's theory or

---

[26] An ordinal scale is one that places items in order without using equal units or an absolute zero.

procedures; but the development of a standardized Piagetian scale of intelligence could change all that. In fact, it might even significantly affect the character of school psychology as a professional discipline. There has been a recent trend away from testing as the prime function of the profession, and toward more involvement in the process of education in the classroom. The new test could precipitate a fusion of those two functions. The school psychologist would be the person in the school who knows the most about how children think, and would be drawn into the classroom as a more active, specialized participant in the educational process.

Finally, a Piaget-inspired scale of intelligence would facilitate basic research on questions of practical concern. "The psychology of the exceptional child," for example, could be expected to have immediate impact on "the education of the exceptional child." It may turn out that reading and writing disabilities can be traced to the distortion of certain fundamental representations, or even of prerepresentational structures, and that the same is true of the more generalized disabilities known as "mental retardation." Programs might be devised for "gifted" children that would take advantage of their gifts without interfering with the harmony and integration of "normal" development. Counselors would profit from a clarification of the nature of aptitudes. And of course everyone in the school would benefit from a deeper understanding of children's thinking in general.

Limitations and Residual Questions

Piaget-inspired theoretical work by now must be acknowledged as reasonably mature, even if the Geneva group is considered in isolation; but the work on applications is in its infancy. I have suggested that applications are possible, I have derived some principles that are relevant to teaching, and I have cited some examples that are relevant to those principles. Most recently, I have described an intelligence test that embodies both the theory and the method of the Geneva group.

For the teacher, several projects are in process right now that promise more or less direct assistance to those who are sophisticated enough to use it. The directness of that assistance runs all the way from experimental studies of teaching in several subject-matter disciplines to a series of "teachers guides."[27]

But regardless of the specific teaching aids that might eventually emerge from all this activity, a genuine professional person can realize an immediate gain by studying the theory itself. A theory may serve as a kind of framework to which both old and new facts may adhere. Or to put it another way, it is like a fisherman's creel; without it, one has no place to put the fish—or the facts—that he catches.[28] Such a framework makes it possible for the teacher to analyze the child in terms of the operations of which he is capable at that particular time and to analyze the task in terms of the operations required to perform it. He might then combine the two in such a way as to produce optimal discrepancy, which would ensure high motivation, much activity, and a maximum of change in cognitive structure. The dedicated teacher may also hope for a gain quite apart from the success of his own interventions in the developmental process: He may hope to attain the kind of satisfaction that comes to the anthropologist who has studied a preliterate culture until he actually understands how its people think.

The ideas that I have presented concerning applications, however, are extremely tentative; and one should not overlook their limitations. In the remainder of this chapter I shall discuss some of these limitations and point to some issues that remain unresolved.

It is not difficult to find a possible limitation to the application just discussed: the amount of time required of a highly competent professional person to test a single child by the Montreal method is truly formidable. Pinard and Laurendeau report that in their standardization project, the average individual testing time was 10 hours.[29] Since that was exploratory work, the figure is probably somewhat inflated; but it is at least indicative of a serious difficulty, especially if the test reports are to be used routinely in the planning of classroom activities. Whether that difficulty will be alleviated by a reduction in testing time or by an increasing in the number of psychological specialists in the schools is a moot question. It is not unreasonable to hope for both.

---

[27] Personal communication from Dr. G. Matthews of the Nuffield Foundation, London, England.

[28] One obvious shortcoming of this analogy is that, unlike a theory, the creel doesn't have anything to say about where to look in the first place.

[29] Adrien Pinard and Monique Laurendeau, "A Scale of Mental Development Based on the Theory of Piaget: Description of a Project," *Journal of Research in Science Teaching*, vol. 2, 1964, p. 257.

Another difficulty is a lack of extensive verification of the success of interventions of various kinds. That lack may be due partly to the immaturity of the intervention procedures. It may also be due to the inadequacy of the testing devices used in their evaluation. Those limitations will be removed in the course of time, but not simply by the passage of time. Efforts like those of Pinard and others with the Montreal intelligence scale will have to be continued and extended. The same is true of interventions like those of Sigel, Roeper, and Hooper, for it must be conceded that although some other successes have been reported, most efforts to induce concrete operations in young children have not been very successful. Perhaps a remedy can be found in the study by Sigel, Roeper, and Hooper: perhaps the answer lies in a more detailed analysis of the operation to be taught. They achieved their success by breaking "conservation" down into lower-order skills and then making each product of the analysis into a subgoal of teaching; when all of the subgoals have been reached, so has the main one (in this case, "conservation").

Studies of the effects of experience on children's thinking are often classified into two groups: (1) physical and quantitative thinking and (2) language and associative processes. Piaget's influence has been largely confined to the first. The reason can be found, of course, in the theory, which often regards language as merely an epiphenomenon. If the theory is modified (as any viable theory must be) that may be one of the modifications; for it seems to me that language can serve both as a device for the deployment of attention and as a mechanism for efficient coding of information. Moreover, although language may sometimes function quite independently, I suspect that it is sometimes an integral part of operational intelligence.

It may be worth noting in this connection that there are in a child's life many occasions for learning that do not contribute in any direct way to operational intelligence. Children must learn very early, for example, to "respect the rights of others." Most kindergarten children never do respect the rights of other people, really, for they are incapable of adopting the other's point of view. But they can be conditioned to discriminate certain stimuli from others, to differentiate some responses from others, and to organize those discriminations and differentiations into patterns that superficially resemble respect for the rights of others. For purposes of efficient administration of groups of children, at home or at school, that may be sufficient; it is at the very least helpful! And so it goes with many other acquisitions. Piaget may not be concerned with them, but that does not mean that the conscientious parent or teacher need not be.

When Piaget does turn his attention toward the practical affairs of the classroom, he sometimes seems to subscribe to what I have called a "recapitulation" sequence of activities in school learning. The teacher "might begin by having the child operate directly on physical entities, then have him proceed to cognitive anticipations and retrospections of operations not actually performed at the moment, and so on, until the originally external actions can take place internally and in complete autonomy from the environment."[30] Although that is a valid account of the series of acquisitions over a period of time extending from the sensorimotor period to the Concrete Operations Subperiod, it may not represent a necessary sequence for every new acquisition of content *within* the Concrete Operations Subperiod or beyond it. In the extreme case, the recapituation model would require that a high school physics student begin his study of mechanics, for example, at the sensorimotor level, continue through the preoperational and concrete operational levels, and only then be ready to deal with the material on a formal level. That would be an extremely inefficient way to teach physics.

Suchman's Inquiry Training has been criticized in much the same vein—that is, the argument has turned on the issue of efficiency. If recapitulation is not necessary, then requiring it of students in the more advanced periods of development may well be inefficient. Specifically, Ausubel has called for a distinction between "reception" and "discovery" learning—i.e., between (1) "the long-term acquisition and retention of stable, organized, and extensive bodies of meaningful, generalizable knowledge" and (2) "growth in the ability to use this knowledge in the solution of particular problems, including those problems which, when solved, augment the learner's original store of knowledge."[31] He points out that although the two may overlap, they are distinguishable, and he asserts further that "the inductive derivation of concepts and generalizations from diverse instances is ... only a conspicuous feature of concept attainment during childhood ...."[32] If

---

[30] John H. Flavell, *The Developmental Psychology of Jean Piaget*, Princeton: D. Van Nostrand Co., Inc., 1963, pp. 368–369.

[31] David P. Ausubel, "Reception versus Discovery Learning in Classroom Instruction," *Educational Theory*, vol. 2, 1961, pp. 21–24.

[32] *Ibid.*, p. 136. Ausubel goes on to say that the acquisition of knowledge is a legitimate objective in its own right and that the goal of the second kind of learning is usually "to facilitate everyday living and decision-making, not to discover knowledge that is of sufficient general significance to merit permanent incorporation in cognitive structure."

Ausubel is right, the Suchman strategy is appropriate to use throughout the Concrete Operations Period but inappropriate thereafter, for it would certainly take an inordinate amount of time to "discover" the enormous amount of "stable, organized, ... meaningful, generalizable knowledge" that must be acquired by anyone who aspires to a general education. Given the motivational advantage of the discovery method, perhaps a compromise of some sort would be in order—a compromise in which discussion begins with the viewing of a discrepant event, but is later guided, to some extent.

My reading of Piaget's theory leads me to suggest that the *kind* of guidance might well vary with the developmental level of the students. It could change from sensorimotor (e.g., requiring that the child perform a particular skilled act) to concrete operational (asking him to predict the results of limited transformations performed within his immediate field of vision) to formal operational (requesting a statement of all possibilities relating to the event). If Ausubel's criticism is to be taken seriously, the *amount* of guidance might vary with the difficulty of the topic under discussion (so that prompts and clues, and even full-blown syntheses, might be included at the higher levels). And at any level (except sensorimotor, of course) Piaget's theory would suggest that the teacher beware of "verbalism"—language performance by the student that gives a false impression of operational facility; the conceptual referents of a given linguistic expression may be strikingly different in a child than they are in his teacher.

Finally, it may not be amiss to take into account Piaget's own attitudes about adult intervention in the process of child development. He has recently expressed himself on two facets of intervention: (1) the amount that is likely to have the most significant effect and (2) the nature of that effect.[33]

Concerning the first of these, his answer seems to be, "Minimal." A statement quoted earlier seems worth repeating here: "Everytime you teach a child something you keep him from reinventing it." We do not know, however, how Piaget would define the word "teach," and we do not know whether he would agree with Ausubel that children and adolescents differ in the amount of "reception" learning that is desirable. It is possible to "teach" without "telling," and it may be that students at different developmental levels differ in the amount of "telling" that they can use.

Even if we grant that intervention can be effective, what is the

---

[33]David Elkind, "Giant in the Nursery—Jean Piaget," *New York Times Magazine*, May 26, 1968, pp. 25–80.

nature of the effect? Specifically, Piaget has addressed himself to the problem of accelerating mental development; and again we find that his attitude is essentially negative. He calls acceleration "the American question," clearly implying that for him it is not a problem at all. To the question "Can we accelerate the stages of development?" Piaget's answer is that we probably can, but that he is not sure that we should. He proffers a "hypothesis"[34] that, he admits, he is so far incapable of proving: that there is an optimal time for the organization of operations. Then he goes on to compare the development of object permanence in a human baby with that same development in a kitten. The child and the kitten go through the same stages; but what requires nine to twelve months in the child is accomplished in three by the kitten. But is that an advantage to the kitten? Piaget says no, that the additional time was not wasted, because the child will continue to develop after the kitten has stopped. There is an optimal time, but the *opti*mal is not *mini*mal. Just what the optimal time is for any given child in any given stage, says Piaget, remains an unanswered question on which we need a great deal of research.[35]

Thus, Piaget's celebrated pessimism reduces to a conviction that the central objective of intervention should be maximal development and that acceleration may not be the best approach to that objective. It is also significant that his statement both begins ("so far incapable of proving") and ends ("need a great deal of research") with a call for further study.

It is perhaps fitting that this book should end with a value judgment and a question for future research. The character of any educational decision depends, after all, upon the values held by the decision-maker and upon the precision with which he can identify his alternatives.

---

[34] "Hunch" might be a better word here, for the idea is not deduced from his theory—or if it is, the deduction is not made explicit.

[35] The statement is from the New York University lectures of March 1967, courtesy of Dr. Frank Jennings. In this same lecture, Piaget asserts that time spent in "hatching an idea," in "simply going around in circles" makes the idea "more stable and fruitful in the long run." It should again be noted that the material from the New York University lectures has been reconstituted from an unofficial record. Dr. Jennings makes no claim of precision, and Piaget has not approved the translation.

Bibliography

This bibliography is intended as a reading list for those students who are motivated to extend their study of Piaget's theory of intellectual development beyond the boundaries that I set for myself when writing this book. Because I assume that most of my readers are fluent only in English, I have cited only the translated version of any contribution that was originally written in another language. Those by Piaget himself have been entirely in French, and not all of them have been translated; hence the list is not complete.* It should perhaps also be noted that Piaget has been a productive worker in fields other than the one that I have chosen to interpret, notably in perception and the development of moral ideas in children. They are all related, of course, and some day may be combined into an integrated theory of cognition; but anyone wishing to inquire into all of them will need to supplement the readings listed here.

---

*The translated works of Piaget and his co-workers are listed chronologically according to the publication date of the French editions.

Almy, Millie, with Edward Chittenden and Paula Miller, *Young Children's Thinking: Studies of Some Aspects of Piaget's Theory*, New York: Teachers College Press, 1966.

Ausubel, David P., "Reception versus Discovery Learning in Classroom Instruction," *Educational Theory*, vol. II, 1961, pp. 21–24.

———, "The Transition from Concrete to Abstract Cognitive Functioning: Theoretical Issues and Implications for Education," *Journal of Research in Science Teaching*, vol. 2, 1964, pp. 261–266.

Beilin, H., and I. C. Franklin, "Logical Operations in Area and Length Measurement: Age and Training Effects," *Child Development*, vol. 33, 1962, pp. 607–618.

Beilin, H., J. Kagan, and R. Rabinowitz, "Effects of Verbal and Perceptual Training on Water-level Representation," *Child Development*, vol. 37, 1966, pp. 317–330.

Birch, H. G., "The Relation of Previous Experience to Insightful Problem Solving," *Journal of Comparative Psychology*, 1945, pp. 367–383.

Boehm, Leonore, "Exploring Children's Thinking," *The Elementary School Journal*, April 1961, pp. 363–373.

Bower, T. G. R., "The Visual World of Infants," *Scientific American*, vol. 215, no. 6 (December 1966), pp. 80–92. [Offprint 502]*

———, "Phenomenal Identity and Form Perception in an Infant," *Journal of Perception and Psychophysics*, 1967, pp. 74–76.

Braine, M. D. S., "The Ontogeny of Certain Logical Operations: Piaget's Formulation Examined by Nonverbal Methods," *Psychological Monographs*, vol. 73, no. 5, 1959. Whole no. 475.

———, "Piaget on Reasoning: a Methodological Critique and Alternative Proposals," in W. Kessen and C. Kuhlman (eds.), "Thought in the Young Child," *Monograph Soc. Res. Child Development*, vol. 27 (2, Serial No. 83), 1962, pp. 41–61.

———, "Development of a Grasp of Transitivity of Length: A Reply to Smedslund," *Child Development*, vol. 35, 1964, pp. 799–810.

Braine, Martin D. S., and Betty L. Shanks, "The Development of Conservation of Size," *Journal of Verbal Learning and Verbal Behavior*, vol. 4, 1965, pp. 227–242.

Brearley, Molly, and Elizabeth Hitchfield. *A Guide to Reading Piaget*, New York: Schocken Books, Inc., 1967.

Brison, D. W., "Acceleration of Conservation of Substance," *Journal of Genetic Psychology*, vol. 109, 1966, pp. 311–322.

Bruner, Jerome S., *Process of Education*, New York: Vintage Books, 1960.

———, "The Course of Cognitive Development," *American Psychologist*, vol. 19, 1964, pp. 1–16.

———, "The Growth of Mind," *American Psychologist*, vol. 20, 1965, pp. 1007–1017.

———, *Toward a Theory of Instruction*, Cambridge: Harvard Univ. Press, 1966.

Scientific American Offprints may be obtained from your bookstore or ordered *by number from* W. H. Freeman and Company, 660 Market Street, San Francisco, California 94104 or Warner House, Folkestone, Kent, England.

———, *Processes of Cognitive Growth in Infancy:* Heinz Werner Lectures, Clark University, Worcester (vol. 3), Barre, Massachusetts: Barre Publishers, 1968.

Bruner, Jerome S., R. R. Olver, P. M. Greenfield, *Studies in Cognitive Growth*, New York: John Wiley & Sons, Inc., 1966.

Charlesworth, William R., "Development and Assessment of Cognitive Structures," *Journal of Research in Science Teaching*, vol. 2, 1964, pp. 215–219.

Cronbach, Lee J., "Learning Research and Curriculum Development," *Journal of Research in Science Teaching*, vol. 2, 1964, pp. 204–207.

Davis, Robert B., "The Madison Project's Approach to a Theory of Instruction," *Journal of Research in Science Teaching*, vol. 2, 1964, pp. 146–162.

Decarie, Therese Gouin, *Intelligence and Affectivity in Early Childhood: An Experimental Study of Jean Piaget's Object Concept and Object Relations*, Translation by P. Brandt and L. W. Brandt, New York: International Universities Press, 1966.

Dingman, W., and M. B. Sporn, "The Incorporation of 8-azaguanine Into Rat Brain RNA and Its Effect on Maze Learning by the Rat: an Inquiry into the Biochemical Basis of Memory," *Journal of Psychiatric Research*, vol. 1, 1961, pp. 1–11.

Dodwell, P. C., "Children's Understanding of Number and Related Concepts," *Canadian Journal of Psychology*, vol. 14, 1960, pp. 191–205.

———, "Children's Understanding of Number Concepts; Characteristics of an Individual and of a Group Test," *Canadian Journal of Psychology*, vol. 15, 1961, pp. 29–36.

———, "Relations Between the Understanding of the Logic of Classes and of Cardinal Number in Children," *Canadian Journal of Psychology*, vol. 16, 1963, pp. 152–160.

Duckworth, Eleanor, "Piaget Rediscovered," *Journal of Research in Science Teaching*, vol. 2, 1964, pp. 172–175.

———, "The Elementary Science Study Branch of Educational Services Incorporated," *Journal of Research in Science Teaching*, vol. 2, 1964, pp. 241–242.

Easley, Jr., J. A., "Comments on the INRC Group," *Journal of Research in Science Teaching*, vol. 2, 1964, pp. 233–235.

Elkind, David, "Giant in the Nursery—Jean Piaget," *New York Times Magazine*, May 26, 1968, pp. 25–27 and 50–57.

———, "The Development of Quantitative Thinking: A Systematic Replication of Piaget's Studies," *Journal of Genetic Psychology*, vol. 98, 1961, pp. 37–46.

———, "Children's Discovery of the Conservation of Mass, Weight, and Volume: Piaget Replication Study II," *Journal of Genetic Psychology*, vol. 98, 1961, pp. 219–227.

———, "The Development of the Additive Composition of Classes in the Child: Piaget Replication Study III," *Journal of Genetic Psychology*, vol. 99, 1961, pp. 51–57.

———, "Children's Conception of Right and Left: Piaget Replication Study IV," *Journal of Genetic Psychology*, vol. 99, 1961, pp. 269–276.

————, "Children's Conception of Brother and Sister: Piaget Replication Study V," *Journal of Genetic Psychology*, vol. 100, 1962, pp. 129–136.

————, 'Discrimination, Seriation, and Numberation of Size and Dimensional Differences in Young Children: Piaget Replication Study VI," *Journal of Genetic Psychology*, vol. 104, 1964, pp. 275–296.

Elkind, David, and John Flavell, *Studies in Cognitive Development: Essays in Honor of Jean Piaget*, New York: Oxford Univ. Press.

Fantz, R. L., "Ontogeny of Perception," *in* A. M. Schrier, H. F. Harlow, and F. Stollnitz (eds.), *Behavior of Nonhuman Primates*, New York: Academic Press, 1965, pp. 365–403.

Feffer, M., and L. Suchotliff, "Decentering Implications of Social Interactions," *Journal of Personality and Social Psychology*, vol. 4, 1966, pp. 415–442.

Festinger, L., *A Theory of Cognitive Dissonance*, Evanston, Illinois: Row, Peterson, 1957.

Flavell, John H., *The Developmental Psychology of Jean Piaget*, Princeton: D. Van Nostrand Co., Inc., 1963.

Furth, H. G., "Conservation of Weight in Deaf and Hearing Children," *Child Development*, vol. 35, 1964, pp. 143–150.

Gagné, R. M., "The Acquisition of Knowledge," Psychological Review, vol. 69, 1962, pp. 355–365.

————, *The Conditions of Learning*, New York: Holt, Rinehart and Winston, 1965.

————, "Curriculum Research and the Promotion of Learning," in *Perspectives of Curriculum Evaluation*, AERA Monograph Series on Curriculum Evaluation, no. 1, Chicago: Rand-McNally, 1967, pp. 19–38.

————, "Contributions of Learning in Human Development," *Psychological Review*, vol. 75, 1968, pp. 177–191.

————, "Learning Hierarchies," Presidential address to Division 15, American Psychological Association, August 31, 1968.

Gagné, R. M., and L. T. Brown, "Some Factors in the Programming of Conceptual Learning," *Journal of Experimental Psychology*, vol. 62, 1961, pp. 313–331.

Gagné, R. M., J. R. Mayor, H. L. Garstens, and N. E. Paradise, "Factors in Acquiring Knowledge of a Mathematical Task," *Psychological Monographs*, vol. 76, no. 526, 1962.

Gagné, R. M., and N. E. Paradise, "Abilities and Learning Sets in Knowledge Acquisition," *Psychological Monographs*, vol. 75, no. 518, 1961.

Gilmary, Sister I. H. M., "Examination of Some of Piaget's Principles in Application to Psychology of Arithmetic," *Catholic Educational Review*, vol. 62, 1964, pp. 369–375.

Goodnow, Jacqueline J., "A Test of Milieu Effects with Some of Piaget's Tasks," *Psychological Monographs*, vol. 76, no. 36, 1962.

Griffiths, Judith, Carolyn Shantz, and I. E. Sigel, "A Methodological Problem in Conservation Studies: The Use of Relational Terms," *Child Development*, vol. 38, no. 3, 1967, pp. 841–848.

Gruen, G. E., "Experiences Affecting the Development of Number Conservation in Children," *Child Development*, vol. 36, 1965, pp. 964–979.

Halstead, W. C., and W. B. Rucker, "Memory: a Molecular Maze," *Psychology Today*, vol. 2, 1968, pp. 38–67.

Harlow, H. F., "The Formation of Learning Sets," *Psychological Review*, vol. 56, 1949, pp. 51–65.

Hebb, D. O. *The Organization of Behavior*, New York: John Wiley & Sons, Inc., 1949.

———, *A Textbook of Psychology*, Philadelphia: W. B. Saunders Co., 1958 (1st ed.), 1966 (2nd ed.)

Held, Richard, "Plasticity in Sensory-Motor Systems," *Scientific American*, vol. 213, no. 5 (November 1965), pp. 84–94. [Offprint 494]

Hood, H. Blair, "An Experimental Study of Piaget's Theory of the Development of Number in Children," *British Journal of Psychology*, vol. 53, no. 3, 1962. pp. 273–286.

Hubel, D. H. "The Visual Cortex of the Brain," *Scientific American*, vol. 209, no. 5 (November 1963), pp. 54–62. [Offprint 168]

Hubel, D. H., and T. N. Wiesel, "Receptive Fields and Functional Architecture in Two Nonstriate Visual Areas (18 and 19) of the Cat," *Journal of Physiology*, vol. 26, 1965, pp. 994–1002.

Hunt, J. McV., *Intelligence and Experience*, New York: Ronald Press Co., 1961.

———, "Piaget's Observations as a Source of Hypotheses Concerning Motivation," *Merril-Palmer Quarterly*, vol. 9, 1963, pp. 263–275.

Hyden, H., "Satellite Cells in the Nervous System," *Scientific American*, vol. 205, no. 6 (June 1961), pp. 62–70. [Offprint 134]

Inhelder, Barbel, "Criteria of the Stages of Mental Development," *in* J. M. Tanner and Barbel Inhelder (eds.), *Discussions on Child Development*, New York: International Universities Press, 1953.

———, "Operational Thought and Symbolic Imagery," *in* P. H. Mussen (ed.), *European Research in Cognitive Development, Monographs of the Society for Research in Child Development*, vol. 30, no. 2, 1965, pp. 4–18.

Inhelder, Barbel, and Jean Piaget, *The Early Growth of Logic in the Child: Classification and Seriation*. New York: Harper and Row, Publishers, Inc., 1964. (Original French edition, 1959.)

———, *The Growth of Logical Thinking from Childhood to Adolescence: an Essay on the Construction of Formal Operational Structures*, translated by Anne Parson and S. Milgram, New York: Basic Books, 1958. (Original French edition 1955.)

Inhelder, Barbel, M. Bovet, H. Sinclair, and C. D. Smock, "On Cognitive Development," *American Psychologist*, vol. 21, 1966, 160–165.

Isaacs, Susan, *Intellectual Growth in Young Children*, New York: Harcourt, Brace & World, Inc., 1930.

Joyce, Bruce and Elizabeth, "Studying Issues in Mathematics Instruction," *The Arithmetic Teacher*, vol. 11, no. 5 (May 1961), pp. 303–307.

Karplus, Robert, "The Science Curriculum Improvement Study-Report to the Piaget Conference," *Journal of Research in Science Teaching*, vol. 2, 1964, pp. 236–240.

Katz, J. J., and W. C. Halstead, "Protein Organization and Mental Function," *Comparative Psychology Monograph*, vol. 20, 1950, pp. 1–38.

Kephart, Newell C., *The Slow Learner in the Classroom*, Columbus, Ohio: Charles E. Merrill Books, Inc., 1960.

———, *Learning Disability*, West LaFayette, Indiana: Kappa Delta Pi Press, 1968.

Kilpatrick, Jeremy, "Cognitive Theory and the SMSG Program," *Journal of Research in Science Teaching*, vol. 2, 1964, pp. 247–251.

Kingsley, R. C., and V. C. Hall, "Training Conservation Through the Use of Learning Sets," *Child Development*, vol. 38, 1967, pp. 1111–1126.

Kintz, B. L., O. J. Delprato, D. R. Mettee, C. E. Persons, and R. H. Schappe, "The Experimenter Effect," *Psychological Bulletin*, vol. 63, no. 4, 1965, pp. 223–232.

Kofsky, E., "A Scalogram Study of Classificatory Development," *Child Development*, vol. 37, 1966, pp. 191–204.

Kohler, Wolfgang, *The Mentality of Apes* (1924), translated from second revised edition by Ella Winter, New York: Vintage Books, 1959.

Kohnstamm, G. A., "An Evaluation of Part of Piaget's Theory," *Acta Psychologica*, vol. 1, 1963, pp. 313–356.

L'Abate, L., "Consensus of Choice Among Children: A Test of Piaget's Theory of Cognitive Development," *Journal of Genetic Psychology*, vol. 100, 1962, pp. 143–149.

Langer, Jonas, "Disequilibrium as a Source of Development," *in* P. H. Mussen, J. Langer, and M. Covington (eds.), *New Directions in Developmental Psychology*, New York: Holt, Rinehart and Winston, Inc. (In press.)

———, "Implications of Piaget's Talks for Curriculum," *Journal of Research in Science Teaching*, vol. 2, 1964, pp. 208–213.

Laurendeau, Monique, and Adrien Pinard, *Causal Thinking in the Child: a Genetic and Experimental Approach*, New York: International Universities Press, 1962.

Lovell, K., "A Follow-up Study of Some Aspects of the Work of Piaget and Inhelder on the Child's Conception of Space," *British Journal of Educational Psychology*, vol. 29, 1959, pp. 104–117.

———, "A Follow-up Study of Inhelder and Piaget's 'The Growth of Logical Thinking,'" *British Journal of Psychology*, vol. 52, 1961, pp. 143–153.

———, *The Growth of Basic Mathematical and Scientific Concepts in Children*, London: Univ. London Press, 1961.

Lovell, K., B. Mitchell, and I. R. Everett, "An Experimental Study of the Growth of Some Logical Structure," *British Journal of Psychology*, vol. 53, no. 2, 1962, pp. 175–188.

Lovell, K., and A. Slater, "The Growth of the Concept of Time: A Comparative Study," *Journal of Child Psychology and Psychiatry*, vol. 1, 1960, pp. 179–190.

Lunzer, E. A., "Some Points of Piagetian Theory in Light of Experimental Criticism," *Journal of Child Psychology and Psychiatry*, vol. 1, 1960, pp. 191–200.

——, *Recent Studies in Britain Based on the Work of Jean Piaget*, London: National Foundation of Educational Research in England and Wales, 1960.

Mason, Herbert L., "Concepts in Biology," *Journal of Research in Science Teaching*, vol. 2, 1964, pp. 244–246.

Mink, Oscar G., "Experience and Cognitive Structure," *Journal of Research in Science Teaching*, vol. 2, 1964, pp. 196–203.

Moore, Omar K., and Alan R. Anderson, "Some Principles for the Design of Clarifying Educational Environments," *in* David Goslin (ed.), *Handbook of Socialization Theory and Research*, Chicago: Rand McNally & Company. (In Press.)

Morgan, J. J. B., and J. Morton, "The Distortion of Syllogistic Reasoning Produced by Personal Convictions," *Journal of Social Psychology*, vol. 30, 1944, pp. 39–59.

Ojemann, R. H., and Karen Pritchett, "Piaget and the Role of Guided Experiences in Development," *Perception and Motor Skills*, vol. 17, 1963, pp. 927–940.

Peel, E. A., "Experimental Examination of Some of Piaget's Schemata Concerning Children's Perceptions and Thinking, and a Discussion of their Educational Significance," *British Journal of Educational Psychology*, vol. 29, no. 2, 1959, pp. 89–103.

——, "Learning and Thinking in the School Situation," *Journal of Research in Science Teaching*, vol. 2, 1964, pp. 227–229.

Piaget, Jean, *The Language and Thought of the Child*, translated by Marjorie Worden, New York: Harcourt, Brace & World, Inc., 1926. (Original French edition, 1923.)

——, *Judgment and Reasoning in the Child*, translated by Marjorie Worden, New York: Harcourt, Brace & World, Inc., 1928. (Original French edition, 1924.)

——, *The Child's Conception of the World*, translated by Joan and Andrew Tomlinson, New York: Harcourt, Brace & World, Inc., 1929. (Original French edition, 1926.)

——, *The Child's Conception of Physical Causality*, translated by Marjorie Worden, New York: Harcourt, Brace & World, Inc., 1930 (Original French edition, 1927.)

——, *The Moral Judgment of the Child*, translated by Marjorie Worden, New York: Harcourt, Brace & World, Inc., 1932.

——, *The Origins of Intelligence in Children*, translated by Margaret Cook, New York: International Universities Press, 1952. (Original French edition, 1936.)

——, *The Construction of Reality in the Child*, translated by Margaret Cook, New York: Basic Books, Inc., 1954. (Original French edition, 1937.)

———, *Play, Dreams, and Imitation in Childhood*, translated by C. Gattegno and F. M. Hodgson, New York: W. W. Norton & Co., Inc., 1951. (Original French edition, 1945.)

———, *The Psychology of Intelligence*, translated by M. Piercy and D. E. Berlyne, London: Routledge & Kegan Paul Ltd., 1950. (Original French edition, 1947.)

———, "Jean Piaget," *in* E. G. Boring, H. S. Langfeld, H. Werner, and R. M. Yerkes (eds.), *A History of Psychology in Autobiography*, Worcester, Massachusetts: Clark University Press, 1952.

———, "How Children Form Mathematical Concepts," *Scientific American*, vol. 189, no. 5 (November 1953), pp. 74–79. [Offprint 420]

———, "The Development of Time Concepts in the Child," *in* R. H. Hoch and J. Zubin (eds.), *Psychopathology of Childhood*, New York: Grune & Stratton, Inc., 1955.

———, *Logic and Psychology* (based on lectures delivered at the University of Manchester, England, in 1952), New York: Basic Books, Inc., 1957.

———, "The Child and Modern Physics," *Scientific American*, vol. 196, no. 3 (March 1957), pp. 46–51.

———, "Development and Learning," *Journal of Research in Science Teaching*, vol. 2, 1964, pp. 176–186.

———, *Six Psychological Studies* (edited by David Elkind), New York: Random House, Inc., 1967.

———, *On the Development of Memory and Identity:* Heinz Werner Lectures, Clark University, Worcester (vol. 2), Barre, Massachusetts: Barre Publishers, 1967.

Piaget, Jean, and Barbel Inhelder, "Diagnosis of Mental Operations and Theory of Intelligence," *American Journal of Mental Deficiency*, vol. 51, no. 3, 1947, pp. 401–406.

———, *The Child's Conception of Space*, translated by F. J. Langdon and J. L. Lunzer, London: Routledge & Kegan Paul Ltd., 1956. (Original French edition, 1948.)

Piaget, Jean, Barbel Inhelder, and Alina Szeminska, *The Child's Conception of Geometry*, translated by E. A. Lunzer, New York: Basic Books, Inc., 1960. (Original French edition, 1948.)

Piaget, Jean, and Alina Szeminska, *The Child's Conception of Number*, translated by C. Gattegno and F. M. Hodgson, New York: Humanities Press, Inc., 1952. (Original French edition, 1941.)

Pinard, Adrien, and Monique Laurendeau, "A Scale of Mental Development Based on the Theory of Piaget: Description of a Project," translated by A. B. Givens, *Journal of Research in Science Teaching*, vol. 2, 1964, pp. 253–260.

———, " 'Stage' in Piaget's Cognitive-Developmental Theory," *in* David Elkind and John H. Flavell, *Festschrift for Jean Piaget*, Oxford Univ. Press. (In press.)

Radler, D. H., and C. K. Newell, *Success Through Play*, New York: Harper & Row, Publishers, Inc., 1960.

Ripple, R. E., and V. N. Rockcastle (eds.), "Piaget Rediscovered: Selected Papers from a Conference on Cognitive Studies and Curriculum Development," *Journal of Research in Science Teaching*, vol. 2, no. 3, 1964.

Rosenthal, Robert, and K. L. Fade, "The Effect of Experimenter Bias on the Performance of the Albino Rat," *Behavioral Science*, 1963, pp. 183–189.

Rosenthal, Robert, and Lenore Jacobson, *Pygmalion in the Classroom*, "Teacher Expectation and Pupils' Intellectual Development," New York: Holt, Rinehart and Winston, Inc., 1968.

Rosenthal, Robert, and R. Lawson, "A Longitudinal Study of Experimenter Bias on the Operant Learning of Laboratory Rats," *Journal of Psychiatric Research*, vol. 2 (2), 1964, pp. 61–72.

Saltz, E., and Irving E. Sigel, "Concept Overdiscrimination in Children," *Journal of Experimental Psychology*, vol. 73, 1967, pp. 1–8.

Schmitt, F. O., "Macromolecular Specificity and Biological Memory," *in* F. O. Schmitt (ed.), *Macromolecular Specificity and Biological Memory*, Cambridge, Mass.: The M. I. T. Press, 1962.

Sigel, Irving E., "Developmental Trends in the Abstraction Ability of Children," *Child Development*, vol. 24, 1953, pp. 131–144.

———, "The Attainment of Concepts," *in* M. L. Hoffman and Lois V. Hoffman, *Review of Child Development Research*, New York: Russell Sage Foundation, vol. 1, 1964, pp. 209–248.

———, "The Piagetian System and the World of Education," *in* David Elkind and John H. Flavel, *Festschrift for Jean Piaget*, Oxford Univ. Press. (In press.)

Sigel, Irving E., and Frank H. Hooper, *Logical Thinking in Children: Research Based on Piaget's Theory*, New York: Holt, Rinehart and Winston, Inc., 1968.

Sigel, Irving E., Annemarie Roeper, and Frank H. Hooper, "A Training Procedure for Acquisition of Piaget's Conservation of Quantity: A Pilot Study and its Replication," *British Journal of Educational Psychology*, vol. 36, 1966, pp. 301–311. (Reprinted in Irving E. Sigel and Frank H. Hooper, *Logical Thinking in Children: Research Based on Piaget's Theory*, New York: Holt, Rinehart and Winston, Inc., 1968.)

Sigel, Irving E., E. Saltz, and W. Roskind, "Variables Determining Concept Conservation," *Journal of Experimental Psychology*, vol. 7, 1967, pp. 471–475.

Smedslund, Jan, "The Acquisition of Conservation of Substance and Weight in Children: I. Introduction." *Scandinavian Journal of Psychology*, vol. 2, 1961, pp. 11–20.

———, "The Acquisition of Conservation of Substance and Weight in Children: II. External Reinforcement of Conservation of Weight and the Operations of Additions and Subtractions," *Scandinavian Journal of Psychology*, vol. 2, 1961, pp. 71–84.

———, "The Acquisition of Conservation of Substance and Weight in Children: III. Extinction of Conservation of Weight Acquired 'normally' and by Means of Empirical Controls on a Balance." *Scandinavian Journal of Psychology*, vol. 2, 1961, pp. 85–87.

——, "The Acquisition of Conservation of Substance and Weight in Children: IV. Attempt at Extinction of the Visual Components of the Weight Concept." *Scandinavian Journal of Psychology*, vol. 2, 1961, pp. 153–155.

——, "The Acquisition of Conservation of Substance and Weight in Children: V. Practice in Conflict Situations Without External Reinforcement." *Scandinavian Journal of Psychology*, vol. 2, 1961, pp. 156–160.

——, "The Acquisition of Conservation of Substance and Weight in Children: VI. Practice on Continuous vs. Discontinuous Material in Problem Situations Without External Reinforcement." *Scandinavian Journal of Psychology*, vol. 2, 1961, pp. 203–210.

——, "The Acquisition of Conservation of Substance and Weight in Children: VII. Conservation of Discontinuous Quantity and the Operations of Adding and Taking Away," *Scandinavian Journal of Psychology*, vol. 3, 1962, pp. 69–77.

——, "The Effect of Observation on Children's Representation of the Spatial Orientation of a Water Surface." *Journal of Genetic Psychology*, vol. 102, 1963, pp. 195–201.

——, "Development of Concrete Transitivity of Length in Children," *Child Development*, vol. 34, 1963, pp. 389–405.

——, "Internal Necessity and Contradiction in Children's Thinking," *Journal of Research in Science Teaching*, vol. 2, 1964, pp. 220–221.

——, "Concrete Reasoning: A Study of Intellectual Development," *Monographs of the Society for Research in Child Development*, vol. 29, no. 2, ser. 93, 1964, pp. 1–39.

——, "The Development of Transitivity of Length: A Comment on Braine's Reply," *Child Development*, vol. 36, 1965, pp. 577–580.

Suchman, J. Richard, "The Illinois Studies in Inquiry Training," *Journal of Research in Science Teaching*, vol. 2, 1964, pp. 231–232.

Szeminska, Alina, "The Evolution of Thought: Some Applications of Research Findings to Educational Practice," *in* P. H. Mussen (ed.) *European Research in Cognitive Development, Monographs of the Society for Research in Child Development*, vol. 30, no. 2, 1965, pp. 47–57.

Tanner, J. M., and Barbel Inhelder (eds.), *Discussions on Child Development: A Consideration of the Biological, Psychological, and Cultural Approaches to the Understanding of Human Development and Behavior* (volume Four of *The Proceedings of the World Health Organization Study Group on the Psychobiological Development of the Child, Geneva, 1956*), New York: International Universities Press, 1960.

Thomson, W. R., and R. Melzack, "Early Environment," *Scientific American*, vol. 194, no. 1 (January 1956), pp. 38–42. [Offprint 469]

Tuddenham, Read D., "Jean Piaget and the World of the Child," *American Psychologist*, vol. 21, March 1966, pp. 207–217.

Uzgiris, Ina C., "Situational Generality of Conservation," *Child Development*, vol. 35, 1964, pp. 831–841.

Wallach, Lise, A. Jack Wall, and Lorna Anderson, "Number Conservation: the Roles of Reversibility, Addition-Subtraction, and Misleading Perceptual Cues," *Child Development*, vol. 38, 1967, pp. 425–442.

Wallach, Lise, and R. L. Sprott, "Inducing Number Conservation in Children," *Child Development*, vol. 35, 1964, pp. 1057–1071.

White, Burton L., "An Experimental Approach to the Effects of Experience on Early Human Behavior," *in* J. P. Hill (ed.), *Minnesota Symposium on Child Psychology* (vol. 1), Minneapolis: Univ. of Minnesota Press, 1967, pp. 201–225.

———, "The Initial Coordination of Sensorimotor Schemas in Human Infants —Piaget's Ideas and the Role of Experience," *in* David Elkind and John Flavell (eds.), *Studies in Cognitive Development: Essays in Honor of Jean Piaget*, Oxford Univ. Press, 1967.

White, Burton L., and Richard Held, "Plasticity of Sensorimotor Development in the Human Infant," *in* Judy F. Rosenblith and W. Alinsmith (eds.), *The Causes of Behavior: Readings in Child Development and Educational Psychology* (2nd ed.), Boston: Allyn and Bacon, Inc., 1966.

White, Stephen, *Students, Scholars, and Parents*, New York: Doubleday & Co., Inc., 1966.

Wohwill, Joachim F., "Developmental Studies of Perception," *Psychological Bulletin*, vol. 57, 1960, pp. 249–288.

———, "A Study of the Development of the Number Concept by Scalogram Analysis," *Journal of Genetic Psychology*, vol. 97, 1960, pp. 345–377.

———, "Piaget's System as a Source of Empirical Research," *Merrill-Palmer Quarterly*, vol. 9, 1963, pp. 253–262.

———, "Cognitive Development and the Learning of Elementary Concepts," *Journal of Research in Science Teaching*, vol. 2, 1964, pp. 222, 226.

———, "Comments in Discussion on the Developmental Approach of Jean Piaget," *American Journal of Mental Deficiency, Monograph Supplement*, vol. 70, 1966, pp. 84–105.

———, "Piaget's Theory of the Development of Intelligence in the Concrete Operations Period," *American Journal of Mental Deficiency, Monograph Supplement*, vol. 70, 1966, pp. 57–83.

———, "The Mystery of the Prelogical Child," *Psychology Today*, vol. 1, 1967, pp. 25–34.

Wohlwill, Joachim F., and R. C. Lowe, "Experimental Analysis of the Development of the Conservation of Number," *Child Development*, vol. 33, 1962, pp. 153–168.

Wolinsky, Gloria F., "Piaget's Theory of Perception: Insights for Educational Practices with Children Who Have Perceptual Difficulties," *Training School Bulletin*, vol. 62, 1965, pp. 12–25.

Woodward, Mary, "The Behavior of Idiots Interpreted by Piaget's Theory of Sensori-Motor Development," *The British Journal of Educational Psychology*, vol. 29, February 1959, pp. 60–71.

———, "Concepts of Number of the Mentally Subnormal Studied by Piaget's Method," *Journal of Child Psychology and Psychiatry*, 1961, pp. 249–259.

———, "Concepts of Space in the Mentally Subnormal Studied by Piaget's Method," *British Journal of Social and Clinical Psychology*, vol. 1, 1962, pp. 25–37.

Zimiles, H., "The Development of Differentiation and Conservation of Number," *Monograph Society for Research in Child Development*, vol. 31, no. 6, 1966. Whole no. 108.

Index